The Doubting Disease:

How one person took charge of the mental disorder that

plagued her decisions for a decade, finally embraced the

unknown, and found the power of choice.

To our Story, and all the Stories to come.

For Marlena

Stories

Prelude

People like to debate other people's truth, but I know this does no good. Someone's truth does not change in light of the words of others. This book is my truth.

I am the weak one. The one who couldn't fight those thoughts when they were big red demons with claws and I, a mere human. The one who cries – a lot. The one who feels. *Everything.* And while I'm sure there are others out there, I walk this road alone. Sure, I can hold hands with another, even share my story with another, but then their power just eats me alive. Their strength swallows me whole.

I am the anxious one. Oh, not that kind of anxiety. Nope, not that either. The anxiety that steals your sleep, burns your dreams, slashes your health. The kind that owns your mind. Not the same, eh? I promise you, it's not. The kind that only comes from a gentle heart and true intentions, traumatized. The kind you can't explain. No, childhood was not bad, and yes, I am even pretty. Smart too.

Those smarts. The part I am proud of, and yet it hurts, God damn it. And using my head to study human behavior and the human mind, of all things? "Too smart for her own good" and "you know too much" has nearly taken my life.

1

But the real confession is the anxiety. It rips away good days, and I can't get them back. Some of the best days of my life, actually. I could feel that I got *everything,* and you know what I hear? That it will go away. She will leave. I will fall, and never succeed. No matter what you fight for, what you EARN, how hard you work on you...it will end. And it will be your fault. That's right - you deserve it. Even the illusion of the mind goes, leaving only what remains. Fear.

This is OCD.

This book took me years to write.

This took me time, and I gave myself time, because telling the story about the worst time of my life, the worst thing that has ever happened takes a lot out of me. I heard once that when you can tell your story without that story "holding" you, you have healed. Well, I am not there as I write this, but much closer than where I was years ago. I believe that one day I will be. But not knowing how long that will take, I remain determined to do what I consider to be my main professional goal in life: to make an impact. To use my experience to help even one person is enough of a motivation to inspire these words to the end.

I am writing this book for no other reason except that I am meant to. I feel it with everything I have that though my life is largely carved with choices I make, this is something else. This is fate. And you can't escape fate; it will chase you down as it has chased me.

I went through this to write these words. That there are people who can write the words and there are people who have felt the experiences, and few people can do both. But I know that I can.

I'll go even further. I feel that I found my interest in psychology at a young age, left that field at 23, came into the field of social work, and even worked with some of the most challenging populations. And then – and this is the worst part, I promise you – I was born with the genetic inclination toward anxiety and my life led me toward experiences that would enhance that to the right degree so that I would develop obsessive-compulsive disorder.

I say "develop" because there are no words for some things. I have had OCD symptoms for as long as I can remember, but it wasn't OCD as we see on TV, with people scrubbing their hands, collecting more belongings than the square footage of their house can hold, and not stepping on cracks.

No, my house isn't so clean you can eat off the floor, and I only take one shower a day. I *throw things out* to a problematic degree, and I would even describe my decorating habits as minimal.

But I have been there. To the depths of the disorder, past the point of words. My obsessions were by the dozens and the compulsions mostly in my head, and I would be lying if I said they were far, far away.

The truth is, they are never that far. I am never that far from slipping, or at least that is how many of us feel. We live life on the edge more than the person who first dubbed this saying can fathom, because if we overthink too long, if we itch too deep, if we *obsess* too much, it can grab us again. We flirt with it every day.

So, I am writing these words for no reason except that I feel I must. I feel I was born to, and just like with the career I chose, I can't run away from the words I am meant to write or speak. My only hope is that with time, the words continue to become less difficult, as they already have.

The truth is, as my 20s went on, I progressively checked out. I was kind of an empty energy that took over while I went somewhere else, and in the last months of that decade, I disappeared completely.

The first thing that I think as I write that is…I hope it doesn't hurt my parents to know how much of it wasn't me, how long it went on. To get help, I had to be as vulnerable as I have ever been and allow the people around me to see just how much pain I was in by letting them inside my dark, sinister head. To write this, I have to be equally vulnerable.

There is something I can say for hitting bottom emotionally, mentally…it all feels the same. Forget feelings, thoughts, whatever is going on…what happens is this: you vacate. You fade away and cannot be reached. I can hardly remember those times, and I truly think that something darker occupies all of us who have felt this.

I have heard this tale so many times before, and as a professional and a person who has been to the depths of both, I am going to set it straight. Anxiety and depression are related, yes, but they are **not the same.** Just as I am as genetically connected to my brother as I'll ever be to anyone, but we are not the same. If a person has felt anxiety, yes, they probably have felt depression. I believe it can even be the same genetic component behind both. But here is the difference.

I had a hormonal imbalance for six long, arduous, **painful** months when I was 25 – I believe, triggered by severe OCD symptoms. This would be my second of three episodes, and the main experience was severe depression. *I felt everything.* I slept a lot. I didn't laugh, I didn't feel joy, and worst of all, I didn't want to live. I barely got dressed to go to work, and as I was a field social worker, I got away with a lot of working from home. I felt nothing from the patients I worked with. I didn't stop eating, as I did with the anxiety. I cried **all** the time. Most of the time, my head was empty, and I could not find a single "bad thought" or reason in my wonderful life to feel the way that I did. Finally, the doctor said he knew exactly why I was depressed and that it was "no wonder."

OCD Brittany felt *nothing.* I hardly slept. I could laugh in the moment, and I did not want to kill myself. I went to work **every single day**, though I had to quit at some point because patients would trigger my anxiety. I could not work with other people's pain for 18 months. I stopped eating, and near the end, I lost 20% of my body weight. I didn't cry every day. My mind never stopped. I was too busy thinking to feel anything. I had a feeling of doom regarding the future and felt something was always coming for me. I was constantly scared, and fear was the only feeling I truly remember.

Anxiety energized me past sanity, depression deflated me past sanity. But in the end, it was the same. I had left the building.

As I came back into myself at 29, I began to grieve the lost time, my lost self. When she had left, I wasn't sure. How much of her was there between my episodes or before age 22 when I experienced my first major episode of OCD? Again, not sure. The only thing I am sure of is that I am here now. Me, sitting here, writing this, finally seeing my life and the world outside of the tunnel I inhabited for so long. I am grateful, but as that gratitude came only through my pain, it is bittersweet.

Denial

I do not weep because
I'm unhappy
I weep because I have everything Yet
I am unhappy

Rupi Kaur

I am a control freak.

It's not what you think. I usually don't care what I eat for dinner, what way I drive to my destination, or even where that destination is. But I care. I care about the things that mean the most to me, and I am scared beyond anything that my mind will devise ways to take them away.

I'm not sure how many people know what it is like to be afraid of their own minds, but it has been my greatest fear in life. Perhaps my only fear. It makes me feel like something is always coming for me. Something that will destroy it all.

In my 29th year, I finally got a name for this terrible thing that hits what I want and love most: obsessive-compulsive disorder. And mine comes with a lovely, self-sabotaging twist.

I grew up wanting to be a doctor. That, I knew, always. That was innately who I was – I wanted to help people. I wanted to always be the strong one in the room. Maybe because I always felt like the weak one in my family. I was the sensitive. The crier, the gullible, the irritable, the one dying to be heard, trying to be understood.

I grew up with strong ideas about what things should be, what I should be. At heart, I was an adventurous, knowledge-hungry person who wanted to affect change more than anything. Who wanted to move mountains, to be educated, to travel. I loved school and wanted to go as far as I could. I wanted to help people.

I also wanted to be paid to read and learn, and never stop. At some point, I realized I could not be a medical doctor due to my weak stomach, so I focused on getting a PhD in counseling after my first psychology class at the age of 14. I wanted my doctorate, and secondly, I wanted a forever partner.

The first time around for both of my wants didn't go so well. When I was 22 years old, I got to the state of Mississippi to finally take my chance at a PhD, and I froze. At the time, I wanted the degree more than I wanted oxygen to breathe. It was more important than my home, my family, my partner, literally everything. I arrived, began my program, and realized suddenly that there were countless things that could get in my way of achieving it. That everything in my life was on the line for a mere chance at completing the PhD. I feared losing my doctorate far too much to have it.

I didn't know the darkest depths of where my fear could go until this point. I never understood fear because everything I had ever feared I had faced and conquered. I feared love, so I went full force and got married at 20. I feared moving away from my family, and so I did. And each of these things I no longer feared once I faced them. But here I was, fearing that I couldn't do it – fearing failure, fearing the loss of what I wanted most. This fear went beyond anything I had ever felt because this time, it was eating away at my mind. The **doubt** I had in myself, in my future was too much for me to handle.

OCD is many things, but fear is a definitive, inherent part. Fear of what will happen, essentially. And in this first severe episode of this OCD fear, away from my family and all I knew, I could only escape it in one way. By giving in to it, bowing to it. By giving up what I wanted most and convincing myself I didn't want it.

My childhood was great in all large senses. I had two parents who had planned me, waited for me, and then cherished my brother and me. It was the unconditional love that all kids should have. They never ceased to want us, love us, and enjoy us. Having a mom who stayed home and a father who taught me the value of hard work, while also being able to balance coming home each evening for dinner, dance lessons, choir concerts, and even bedtime reading, gave me a stability and predictability I believe that every child needs to have a sense of trust and security inside this big, scary world.

Best yet, they protected me. Having spent my career listening to horrifying tales of the brothers, fathers, babysitters, neighbors who would hurt children, I am so thankful that my mother, specifically, was so aware of where I was, who I was with, and really, had never allowed much possibility of someone hurting me. Today, people focus on the amount of money they are bringing in and the things they could buy. Kids are more like ornaments, brought into the world as accidents, and treated like inconveniences. People start thinking about who will watch and basically raise their children when the children are already here. Nothing is planned, not even children, and thus, parents are left to do the "best" they can do, last minute, without enough thought.

It seems to me that many people live in a fantasy world that, clearly, my parents knew nothing about. A world where their children would be healthy, happy, and safe for all of time. Where they could go to friends' houses and remain safe. Run around the neighborhood and remain safe. Travel on school trips and remain safe. Watched by uncles or in houses with the older boyfriends of their other children and remain safe. That world, my family and I knew nothing about. My mother knew what could happen to kids, and due to this, I was also very aware of potential dangers growing up. Probably too aware. With my inclination for anxiety and ability to overthink at a very young age, it encouraged a sadness I've always had.

Now a licensed therapist, I would say that I have always coped with a kind of dysthymia – a low-level but never-leaving sadness – as far back as I can remember. I would pass the dull time, month to month, by looking forward to the next holiday, birthday, field trip, Harry Potter book release, and day to day within the stories I would read. I was constantly learning and then informing other people about what I had learned. One day, I gave my mom a lesson about what eating disorders were, and how some people choose to throw up what they eat. I was always a little grown up, reading books or watching things way beyond the maturity or reading level I was at, and sometimes getting in trouble for it. When I misbehaved – usually consisting of reading a book during school lessons, using a curse word, or forthright honesty – my parents would confiscate my bookshelf or threaten to keep me from school.

School was my outlet. Outside of the years that OCD stripped me of all feeling, I always looked forward to learning. I would go to school, come home, and finish my weekly homework on Mondays, do projects weeks ahead of the due dates, and then write my own novels and build my own math workbooks – creating hundreds of problems and then solving them. I loved numbers almost as much as I loved words. What I didn't really know is that numbers weren't just an interest or passion – it was an obsession. And counting, the compulsion.

Looking back, I would say that the greatest barrier to growing up to be an adult who could respond in a healthy way to the things that would happen to me was the anxiety and constant hypervigilance in my household. My mother had been raised in a strict Catholic Italian and very authoritarian household, and she reflected much of this in her expectations. There was no such thing as "cleaning our rooms" because *they were never anything but perfect.* Our beds were made, drawers perfectly aligned, socks folded, bathroom sinks wiped after every use, fingernail polish never peeling, hair done, a cup always with a coaster. My house had four people until my cousins began to live with us intermittently (who also did not have a choice but to keep their rooms pristine), and none of us were anything but neat and clean. Nature or nurture, it didn't matter – it was not an option. It just was.

Most of this was easy for me to comply to, as I loved arranging and organizing things. My mom liked the picture frames halfway between the back and front of tables – I liked them in the back corner, out of the way – so we would compulsively take turns "righting" the frames to our own needs. Bedtimes were always strict and far earlier than that of my peers. I never got anything less than fantastic grades, and I never required homework help or a parent to check it was done. Not once.

This was good, because one of many rules my parents had is that we were going to college and graduating with a bachelor's degree. The end. It was one of the "no ifs, ands, or buts" in our lives. I hated all the rules in my house, but this one I truly never battled. My parents worried about school for my brother, but for me, they had different worries.

I have always been deep and intense – an old soul, my parents called it. If not talking about some taboo subject even adults didn't want to hear about – no less talk to a child about – I was hooked into some fantasy book where children were the heroes. I wanted to believe I could do things in the world, that I could become someone, and maybe even that I already was someone.

I was the kid that wanted to take in any stray. Bad attitude, big heart. I wanted the injured animals, came home with the "different" kids from school, and always volunteered with a needy population. If I saw something or someone who needed some extra love, I took it upon myself to give it. At 12, I supported and encouraged an acquaintance at school to go to our guidance counselor to report her stepfather for sexually abusing her. Earlier, I had asked my parents if we could adopt a cat with a missing leg. My parents knew I would marry someone older, and they were right. I didn't care for the superficiality of the things others did; even later, I never became interested in parties or drinking or sex or anything most teens or young adults would concern themselves with at some point. Anything I did do in these areas were out of peer pressure or curiosity.

My heart left me as a target to the wrong people, and on occasion, the wrong things because I was with the wrong people. I was gullible, just like my mom, and it left me in relationships at times that were harmful. And with parents who really did not know any better.

When I was 12, I was obsessed with the excitement of an online friend I had made. I was fanatic about Harry Potter at that time (which I admit, never left), and I somehow was exposed to an online friend who claimed to be the young actress, Emma Watson. I, of course, had my **doubt**s at first, but after some time and some checks on certain facts, I began to believe it.

I think that being gullible ran in my household. Despite her vast knowledge of "what was out there," I think my mom too believed I was friends with the real actress. It's a better thought than believing that she felt it completely harmless to be friends with a no-name, faceless person on the internet, which was the case.

The internet was a newer and emerging household product in these days, however, and the dangers that most people are aware of today certainly were not common knowledge back then. At a time when most houses did not have a computer, and our one computer sat in the middle of our kitchen, I became friends with an internet predator. One who would never touch or hurt me physically, but instead, altered my reality, hurting me mentally and emotionally.

Years into this relationship, I found out it was a girl named Bethany – a girl like myself who lived in a fantasy world just like I did, where she was anything but just an ordinary girl pretending to be someone famous. Much, much later, I found out that this girl had had cancer, and that she had died, explained to me after the fact by another friend of hers I also met on the internet. A friend who, supposedly, was also deceived by her. This friend, in our daily relationship, took Bethany's place. The mutual loss and betrayal drew me into this friend of hers, probably very much a suave and duplicitous move on this person's part. We both comforted each other, grew to trust each other, and achieved a solid friendship I depended on. I grieved a fake person, then a sick person, then a dead person, never knowing until years later it was probably the very person I was speaking to for almost a decade who was the master mind of the entire thing. That it wasn't three people turned two then one. It was always one.

This friend was a middle-aged man who lived in England. This, I know for sure, because we met in person when I was 15 years old.

My parents picked me up early one day from my first job. When they did, they had him in the back seat. He had contacted my mom (who he also emailed consistently by this time) to say he would be a few hours away and to see if we wanted to all meet up. He was in his 40s and very, very quiet throughout the drive and meal. I was incredibly uncomfortable with this suddenly in-person relationship that everybody involved thought I would be excited about. I was excited only when it was over, and we never met in person again.

My family, again, is gullible. Like I said, they knew what was out there and always considered it, and in this experience, they also considered that them being involved and a conspirator in this relationship would keep this man from "trying anything" with a girl who was *very* well-protected. And they were right, in that sense. He never had the opportunity to physically try anything. However, my parents are very different from me. They never considered what it could possibly do to my mind, my thoughts, or emotions. Sticks and stones, but not words…just another way I was different from the people in my house, in a way they didn't understand. I was very, very sensitive.

The electronic relationship continued for a few more years. To this day, due to the seeming innocence of the encounter, I'm just not sure exactly what was going on. It wasn't until I began therapy around the age of 26 that this event came up again.

Of the handful of people who I have told about this situation, all have had the same reaction: confused horror and anger. Later, in therapy, I would have a strong feeling that inappropriate things were said in these interactions, but I don't have memory of what they were. I do think a basic sense of trust was violated during those years, but it wasn't the trust in adults or people that was in disrepair. It was the trust I had in myself, which would take another hit during my later divorce. However, I am grateful for the good way it did change me…it has gifted me with the ability to accurately perceive other people.

This was the first and only time I felt truly fooled by someone. After this, I trained myself to really know people. Not just to see or hear them, but to feel them. Instinct isn't a precise gift for me; it is a black and white one. You know when it's danger, but you don't know how, or when, or where. You just must trust that it is. To this day, people tell me that I have a sixth sense about people. My mom told me once that I could meet someone and hate them, and it would be years later before *other people* realized that they were very "hateable." That they were not a *good* person. But broken people – that, I don't sense so well, and sometimes, they are one in the same.

––––––––––

As I got older, the thoughts that if I didn't flick switches or push buttons or flush the toilet a certain way or number of times transformed into more sinister ones. It became the thought that if I don't have exactly one scoop EACH of the vanilla, chocolate, and strawberry ice creams we always had – the latter two of which I hated - that something bad would happen. That if I stepped on the pavement crack or touched the tiled countertop cracks we had, something worse would happen. Someone would die. I didn't pay these thoughts enough mind to be upset, because it was easy enough to adhere to them then. Until it wasn't.

———————

When I was 15, I was caught stealing from a department store. I have no idea how it all started, but I know my friend was doing it prior to me and somehow, I began to steal as well. I was very uncomfortable with this habit; after all, how would the bright future I was planning look if after the age of 17 – when I would be considered a legal adult - I was caught? When I got caught, I had been doing it for months, and for me, it had become a compulsion. I had to do it, or I would obsess and become anxious about not doing it. It really isn't until now that I understand this to be kleptomania.

Kleptomania is not stealing. It is the compulsive urge to steal. It is the feeling that one must steal to rid of negative emotions one feels. The stealing was a short period of my teenage years, less than a year, and I did not think of it this way when I was doing it. I thought it was a hobby, and it didn't really violate my "right vs. wrong" boundaries, as my sense of morality has always been focused on not hurting actual people, and I didn't perceive the businesses' losses as harm. I wasn't proud, I wasn't ashamed, I was just scared. And when I did stop, my fear increased. I realized stopping was not just stopping. It was not that simple. Thankfully, I learned to live with the anxiety I felt after stopping, and I never stole another thing.

But obsessions and compulsions continued. If I didn't take the long way driving, my dad would die. I believed that I had to prepare for everyone I loved to die – if I did, it would not actually happen. OCD is irrational. It's a cycle that we don't know how to get out of, and yet, it keeps us going. Images of death and fear became compulsions – I feared if I didn't compulse in whatever way that my mind devised, the images would become real and no longer be merely images. And yet, the compulsions didn't stop them. They always came back.

I knew none of this. I didn't even think twice about these patterns. I simply would obsess and then do exactly what I thought I needed to do to make the thoughts and anxiety stop, until it started again. But I was a kid, and I knew no other reality. Nobody ever noticed or asked what was going on in my mind, and I wouldn't have thought to bring it to anyone's attention.

Here's the thing with kids. They only know one reality until they are shown or educated about another. I was raised with one parent who kept the imperfect, dirty, dark things inside of them until it was too difficult, and then they would let those things out, very unprocessed and unrefined. The other parent would word vomit those things instead. Rather than managing feelings, one parent would explode from them, and the other constantly externalized anxiety, which was felt by the rest of us. Especially me, I think, as I was the most sensitive. Rather than being responsible for managing emotions, I was expected to consider the *emotions* of not only myself, but my parents, while they did not manage their own emotions. It was my responsibility to not "make" my mom worry, "make" my mom anxious, or "make" my dad angry. Today, I understand my parents in clinical terms – a reason I encourage labels. Labels help us understand and accept other people.

I don't say this because it is terrible. In fact, it is normal. Most families are far from perfect. These behaviors weren't going to produce a child who prostituted, or committed felonies, or was a sociopath. I say this, instead, because this was the perfect breeding ground for an anxiety disorder. Constantly having to worry about "how I would make everyone else feel" and what could "possibly happen" as a child was stressful. In these ways, I'm not sure I was ever a kid. But it sure did train me to pick up on the emotions of others.

I would have anxiety and panic attacks every spring starting when I was young. We guessed that pressures of school and wanting to be perfect wore me down emotionally, and I would panic. These panics became full-blown attacks around 15. As usual, I was comforted and convinced I was fine. Anxiety, no matter how intense, was "normal" in my family. Something to merely live with. "Go clean something," mom still says. Severe anxiety can't clean, I would say. It can barely breathe.

When I would get stressed, which was always about school in those years, I would get anxious and go into emotional overload and break down. I didn't have the experiences of bullying, neglect, or abuse, but instead, something invisible. I was processing the obsessive, demeaning, negative thoughts I would have. Worrying about my family, my friends, my future and thus, my grades. I would worry I wouldn't get an A and it would become *You will fail. You will have to retake the class. You won't get into the college you want. You won't do great on the SATs and then you'll be stuck.* This was the beginning of the years that my anxiety would grow more severe and remain unchecked.

Forever the martyr, the young relationships I had were always with someone with a problem. A big problem. Boyfriends with deadly anger, psychotic disorders, and suicidal ideation was all I knew. And when I married, I thought I was finally with someone safe, stable, predictable. Actually, I loved who he was, and that's why I married him. Later, I found out more about traumas he had suffered and how that affected him on a day-to-day basis. cn when it was unconscious, I found those in need.

Later, when fighting off growing symptoms of OCD, I was consistently told by my family that I created my own problems. Being in constant **doubt**, this only fed my self-**doubt** and pushed me further away from treatment. After all, the doctors had no clue why I couldn't stop asking for reassurance, why I was skin picking, why I couldn't sleep from horrific anxiety, why I laid awake at night thinking about the past relationships of my fiancé. But the conclusion I lived with for years was that I was neurotic, anxious, and created my own problems.

Because of this sense of responsibility for my own problems, one diagnosis that I was given was hypochondriasis – DSM-V-TR name of "illness anxiety disorder." After all, I constantly worried that I had a serious mental illness. It sure felt like I had one. Little do most people know that hypochondriasis is not worrying you would get an illness, as I did – it is *believing* you have an illness.

The whole time, little did I know, I did have a mental illness that would one day be severe. It wasn't just worry. But it would be years before it was confirmed. It would take three therapists, even more doctors, my money, my career, my sanity, and nearly my to-be second marriage before anyone believed me, and by then, I didn't even believe me.

Prodromal

You must give up the life you planned in order to have the life that is waiting for you.

Joseph Campbell

What years before had been a sort of crisis of identity, a spiritual awakening, a change of heart, I would later always remember to be my first major obsessive-compulsive episode. For me, OCD thoughts were always consistent, but the intensity of the symptoms waxed and waned over the years, the worst of them always triggered by outside events.

I dropped out of my PhD program in psychology in my first year of study. I was 22 years old, self-confident, and up until the point when I started grad school, a "perfect" student. When I left, I was 23 years old, lost, and defeated. I thought that school had defeated me, and I would carry the disappointment deep within me for years to come. But the truth was, something had gotten to my mind, something so terrifying that it had scared me away from the very thing I would have sacrificed *anything* for.

A goal in writing this book is gathering information for the readers. I want to create a description of common sets of experiences regarding lifelong obsessive-compulsive disorder. This book aims to allow understanding in all people of the mental breakdown that all too commonly precedes the breakdown of a life.

This book serves to support, and not only to support people who have OCD, professionals studying or treating OCD, or families afflicted. It intends to support a larger conversation regarding mental health. A conversation about the consequences of not only the illnesses themselves, but the lack of awareness and effective treatment of them.

This book intends to display the real feelings involved in hitting bottom, at the victim of severe mental illness. We all have our own perceptions of what "bottom" could be. Some people have hit it. For some, their divorce was their bottom. Or the loss of a child. Or maybe even a financial bottom that put them on the streets. Perhaps, an addiction (which I align with mental health breakdowns). It can mean so many things for so many people, and we can hit it more than once. The bottom of a mental illness rips you of your reality, your passions, your feelings, and eventually, your identity. "Bottom" doesn't have a set definition; it is a set of feelings of hopelessness, despair, and so much more. Sometimes, bottom is somewhere we put ourselves. Other times, bottom hits us in the face, unavoidably. Bottom is not having nothing. It is feeling nothing.

Due to the calculated nature of OCD, I hit bottom three times in my 20s. The first time the disorder that had infiltrated my life for as long as I can remember became severe was when I entered my PhD program. The overwhelming anxiety that began turned into a depression when I would fall into my distorted mind, believing and becoming the thoughts that dominated it. Convinced so thoroughly that I would never, ever achieve my PhD, I left it behind.

Earning admission into a fully funded PhD program dominated my life throughout high school and college. I didn't party. I didn't participate when my roommates had friends over. I didn't do drugs. I didn't get wasted. There were only a few times I stayed out all night long. Lucky for me, I also was never interested in any of those things. I got married at 20 to someone older than myself, someone stable and well past the lifestyle of those my age. Someone who accepted that in a year's time, I – and thus, we – would be living in some unknown part of the country, wherever a school would accept me as their doctoral student.

Helping others fulfills me, and I never thought twice of doing it in any other way than becoming a psychologist. I'm one of the few people who never once changed majors in college. I only added them. I began as a psychology major, and realizing I had the time to dual degree, I took up English out of a passion for writing.

I applied to 8 different PhD programs, and when I didn't get into one, I did a third undergraduate degree in Criminal Justice as I waited to apply again. I was told that I was the only person in the history of the university to earn three degrees in the four years of my undergraduate studies, and I had to gain approval from the university president to do so. Somewhere in there, I also did a minor in sociology and a certificate in Women's Studies. I carried two jobs, interned at various agencies, and completed numerous certifications in various areas of my field.

The second year I applied, I submitted applications to 16 programs, spending thousands on the applications alone. I held my breath and put myself through interviews in four different states, experiences that nearly claimed my sanity due to the obvious anxiety. When something important was on the line, my anxiety had always made me nearly unfunctional. I had dyed my hair dark to look serious for the professors and taken the lip ring out of my face and earrings out of my ears. I had pretended I was single (or I should say, omitted that I was married, with the thought that maybe I'd have lesser chance of acceptance if they knew they also had to hope a spouse would want to move as well). 182 credits, four years of school and work, 24 applications, and 4 in-person interviews later, I got the chance. I was accepted to 3 programs, and I chose the program that would look the best for my future (not necessarily the one I wanted or in the place I most wanted to live).

For the first time ever, I was challenged. I was doing advanced statistics, and it was a nightmare. When you aren't used to struggling, you begin to question whether you are in the right place. I began to question if I could get through my program. Looking back, it was not a question as much as a **doubt** – I could definitely have gotten through the program. But I couldn't be sure, and this began to eat away at me.

My intrusive thoughts of the bad things that were going to happen planted themselves, and the overwhelming **doubt** I had in myself and in my future was too much to bear. I wouldn't understanding what was happening to my mind for another 7 years, and all I could think was…*Where would I be without my continued academic success, without becoming a doctor? What if something got in the way of it? What if someone dies, and I can't emotionally manage? What if they recant my offer? What if I'm not good enough?*

What if I fail when I am 4 years along?

What if my dissertation gets rejected?

What if I can't get through my classes?

What if I get stuck in year three?

Or stuck on my dissertation, and thus stuck in Mississippi for a decade?

And worst of all, *what if this anxiety never stops?*

This questioning *crippled* me. The fact that I could even question what had always been my dream was completely insufferable. After all, I was a bleeding liberal living in the deep south for this program. *I wanted this that bad.* I began to **doubt** and fear that I would fail, or somehow lose this opportunity so intensely that I wished I *would* lose it just to end the **doubt** and fear.

I had panic attack after panic attack, a dozen per day, and even woke up in the middle of the nights in a full panic. The self-defeating, **doubt**ful thoughts had begun, and I was convinced that I had to leave. I had to drop out of the program. If I didn't, the **doubt**ing would never stop. It was like my compulsion to steal all over again. I couldn't *not* steal because of the feelings that were there when I didn't. I began to believe that I would never be healthy until I left the program, and that this was all a sign. Hence, in my deluded mind, anxiety was a sign that I had to give up all the efforts I had made – that me leaving was "meant to be."

I convinced myself that the **doubt**s were signs and dropping out wasn't a choice. That God was making these feelings of despair happen so I would leave. My OCD was trying to rip away what mattered most to me, for the first time. And I handed it right over. I was completely delusional.

When I first started having obsessive **doubt**s, my family pushed me to stay and to be positive. They thought that I was just freaking out. At first, so did I. They were frightened that I would give up something I had hoped and worked for throughout my life. And that I would regret it. They pushed me hard. To get up in the morning. To make an effort. To be positive. To do my homework. To get dressed. Every time I heard one of them say that I needed to

33

suck it up and do it, something inside me died. As others who have been in similar situations know, it is harder when you feel bound to the people you love, the people you have involved in the process. I felt I *needed* them to understand. I *needed* the reassurance and support to drop out, and this became compulsive. As I would years later in recurring episodes, I called every single person I had ever known in those months I considered leaving my program, under the pretense of seeking advice. But truly, to get validation and reassurance for my already-made decision to leave.

Looking back, I am no longer in regret that I left my psychology program, as I later completed a doctorate in a field more suited to me. But my regret is around *why* I left – it was the obsessions about the future, it was the **doubt** and fear of what would happen, and it was the complete inability to handle the anxiety that resulted. When I considered leaving, the anxiety and panic would ease. But intrusive thoughts continued, and in feeling that leaving was the only way that I could escape the anxiety from my **doubt**ing, I became depressed, feeling I had no choice. I could not give the program a real chance, because I literally could not survive the level of anxiety I felt in staying. I was living inside my own head, and it was a dark, sinister place I could not continue to endure.

Graduate programs are ideal breeding grounds for obsessive-compulsive disorder. The need to be perfect is real, and the possibility of failure never far. Graduate school can be impossibly challenging. Until I was in this program, I did not know the meaning of "pressure." I went from being in the top 2% of my high school class (of 900 students) to getting three bachelor's degrees and more work experience than most people have in a lifetime to a place where *everyone else was just as impressive as me.* We were all straight-A students. Some had gone to Ivy League schools. Others came from families of doctors and lawyers. The pressures are beyond what can be described with words because the worst of the pressure is what we do to ourselves. It is inside each overachiever, and deeper than therapy or drugs can relieve.

In my PhD program, I was in fearful turmoil. Without it, I was suicidal. Being a grad student – even just planning for it for years, as I had - does something to your expectations, something to your mind. Just my effort to get into grad school, making it everything I wanted in life, did something to my own mind. It was the hardest thing I have ever had to give up. And yet, without it, I saw black.

Suicide is the second leading cause of death among adolescents and college students. The University of Michigan estimates that 26 percent of their students consider suicide. Even for those who enter college as mentally healthy, many succumb to the pressures, the isolation, the confusion unique to higher education.

I have always thought a certain way about suicide. I empathize with it, and I understand some of the feelings that go along with it, but I always figured that anything that somebody runs from now, they are going to have to face eventually. It is not a matter of heaven and hell, as I don't believe in these dimensions in the same manner that many people do, but it is a matter of learning. I am a very spiritual person, and to me, life is just a short period of learning. Anything we do here will be carried with us later. Suicide is not the end, it is only the beginning of a new dimension, and it is the giving up of further experiences we are meant to have and learn from. Taking that away is a regression in our process of learning.

Only these beliefs saved me from suicidal consideration at this time. I thought about it, as perhaps is natural when one feels so trapped and pained, but I think some of us would never kill ourselves due to some foundational beliefs that go right to our core. But it did scare me. The point when I sought therapy seriously was when I began desiring crashing my car whenever I would drive. I had never in my life had thoughts such as these. But they were suddenly attacking me, especially in the moments when I had time to think.

Sometimes in life, we feel like we can see ahead for years. And other times, we can barely make out what is in front of us. I have never been one who has allowed it to get dark…I have not been comfortable with darkness, with not knowing what was to come for me. So, I have filled my surroundings with an artificial light of "knowing" at all times. Sometimes I didn't even have back-up plans because back-ups meant I was unsure what would happen, and I always made sure I knew my future. I only needed one plan, which was going to happen no matter what. After dropping out of my PhD program, I avoided anything that challenged me, so I never had to question myself again. Thus, never being truly challenged again. For me, **doubt** meant mental breakdown; unconsciously knowing this, I laid low inside my own life. I settled. In school, in marriage, in location, in life. Contentment is what I grasped, as it would not intimidate my mind. On the outside, I seemed a success, but on the inside, I was playing it safe.

Ending

Be patient toward all that is unsolved in your heart and try to love the questions themselves, like locked rooms and like books that are now written in a very foreign tongue. Do not now seek the answers, which cannot be given to you because you would not be able to live them. And the point is, to live everything. Live the questions now. Perhaps you will then gradually, without noticing it, live along some distant day into the answer.

Joseph Campbell

I wanted a partner for life. I wanted the impermeable bond my parents had, and mostly, I wanted safety. My prior relationships had been tumultuous and devastating, and I needed stability. So, I married someone who was safe, predictable, reliable. Someone I could trust.

While I was consumed with my own emotional issues and decision-making in Mississippi, my spouse was over-working – a habit that would never cease and only grew more problematic with time. I felt that this along with a refusal to work on the marriage made it impossible to better our unhappy marriage. This is when the deterioration of the relationship really began.

He and I were two very different people, unhappy from the beginning. I feared losing stability, I feared hurting him, and mostly, I wanted to avoid the self-hate of failing a marriage. Marriage is sacred to me, and I meant the vows I had taken more than anything. So, despite all that would happen, I settled and accepted the reality of the relationship.

OCD can be psychotic. During the time in my PhD program, the heaviness of the depression, the fear, and the anxiety led me to believe my thoughts were prophetic. And it would not be the first time. Of course, I didn't really voice this to others…who *does* voice the deepest of their spiritual thoughts and beliefs to other people? I thought I had had a spiritual enlightening. For years, I would even attend retreats, learn palmistry, and take mediumship classes. I enjoyed it, not knowing that these were not the safest explorations for someone with unhinged, undiagnosed OCD. My OCD would take the form of an energy that showed its face when there was something to dispose of. In other words, when I found something wonderful, it prepared to get rid of it.

OCD would claim my 20s. Largely being the cause of my part in the dissolution, it will forever have my first marriage, the joy of earning my degrees, and the travel I should have enjoyed more in that time. At the times that I should have made more effort, I could not, and inside that relationship, I would never be able to, largely stuck inside my own head. I am still claiming back some of the self-love that disappeared as well. In the years that should have been exciting, bright, and interesting, I was tired, alone, and anxious. Until the edge of 30, OCD would present itself when something important was on the line. It would become severe when I had something in my life that gave me purpose, something that was *very important*. I would learn too late that it had never left; it was only hiding sometimes.

The month I was graduating with my master's degree in social work at the age of 25, the obsessions began again, hard and fast. This time was worse, as I not only dealt with the depths of anxiety and helplessness, but I also felt an intense depression that set in harder and just as quickly as the anxiety had.

It was the day before Easter. I had just finished re-reading the Harry Potter series, which I read every few years. This time, I began feeling the way I felt when I was a young girl reading the books. I remembered the dreams I had had, who I wanted to be, and mostly, my desire to be a doctor. This feeling of despair that came with the **doubt**s regarding the life I was living sunk in fast.

A large, suppressed part of me knew I had made mistakes in the most important areas of my life. That I had married too young and given up what I wanted most for it. Today, I am grateful that I was married to someone who is today one of my best friends. But in marriage, we both felt trapped trying to fit each other. I was a dreamer, not just regarding life, career, travel, but also relationships. I wanted to learn, grow, and overall, do better. I wanted to talk and ponder and wonder and make plans. I wanted to read and always be looking for my dream job.

In marriage, we must make sacrifices. As I said, I took my marriage vows as seriously as anyone does. At the time, my spouse sacrificed by moving for my education, and in moving back home, I knew that my sacrifice had to be the doctorate degree that I wanted more than anything. We needed to stay in Florida where his job was. I could not ask him to sacrifice more. This was before a wide array of doctoral degrees were available online, and none were offered in our area. And even if I could get my doctorate, the knowledge that I would surely have to move in order to use it the way I probably would want to, as a professor, kept me rooted to reality. It was my marriage or my dream, and I chose my marriage. And at the back of my mind the entire time, I also believed that my mind would likely sabotage any chance I got.

In this sacrifice, in settling in both marriage and career, it all hit me when reading the Harry Potter books again. What I had wanted as a child, the dreams I had always had when reading them all those times before. I became severely depressed as I overthought and over-regretted, constantly stuck in my head. I obsessed about what I wished had been, the marriage I wished I had, and the opportunity I wished I had not given up three years before – the opportunity I had worked so hard for. In this episode, my compulsions of reassuring myself and talking back to the thoughts were mostly in my head. The checking, the symmetry, the thoughts of death remained, always, and now they were coupled with the same kind of obsessive self-deprecation that I had experienced years before. The result this time was more so depression than anxiety, and given the disinterest in my life, it makes sense why. But then, I did not understand why I was feeling the way I was.

I spent five months going to doctors, psychics, talking to anyone who would listen. You see, I grew up in a household that would not have even *considered* medication. Nope, no way. Some things that we grow up with are much deeper than the mind can rationalize. I wasn't necessarily against medication, but I also wanted a name for what I was dealing with and why I was dealing with it, prior to accepting treatment. I didn't believe I was suddenly "someone who suffered from depression" at the age of 25. And I was right. While I was suffering from a major depressive episode, this was not the root of the issue.

Looking back, I believe those doctors should have recommended medication, given how depressed I was. I think an anti-medication stance with any patient whose symptoms would be labeled "severe" in what they are experiencing is unethical, and potentially malpractice. In fact, if more people would open their minds to the possibility of medication's assistance, I think a lot of lives would be saved. When I eventually – almost five years later - would get on the appropriate medication, my only regret would be that I didn't take it earlier.

The way my mind worked and seemed to *cause* these feelings did not seem like typical depression and anxiety to me. Five months in, I went into an alternative medicine doctor's office. I had hormone panels and heavy metal tests and comprehensive blood panels. I told the doctor that if he did not find what was wrong with me – if he did not find something – I would jump off a bridge.

I'm not sure if I would have done it, but I was at the end of my rope, again. I had decided I would not force myself to live with the level of unexplained despair I felt. It was probably my way of communicating to a professional that I had nothing left in me. This time, it had gone on for months – this almost psychotically superstitious depression and anxiety. I was convinced it was some internal reckoning, something I had to overcome, find the answer to. But I had had enough. I was tired.

There are a handful of periods throughout my episodes that I would become so tired, so sleepless, so helpless that I seemed to shoot into depression. Every time, I was filled with relief. Don't get me wrong, depression is brutal. But it's silent. It's still. It's empty. Anxiety is a loud, frenzied torture.

The tests that the doctor ran can be viewed as somewhat arbitrary, but two major things were found: my serotonin levels were low (neurotransmitter linked to depression), and I had basically no progesterone (a necessary hormone that works with estrogen). I immediately began taking about $600 a month of supplements, and within two weeks, I was on my way to feeling my version of normal.

To this day, I am not fully sure where it all ties together. However, I believe that the obsessive thinking shot me into a depression, and over time, the chronic depression affected my hormones and neurotransmitters. And according to the doctor, my heart, though I don't remember the specifics of why he was concerned for a heart attack. Fixing the hormones and taking these natural anti-depressants led to my recovery. I also, on some level, knew I was at the end of my efforts; going up was the only direction I could move. It could also have simply been the end of the episode. I would rest easier for the next three years.

My fear going forward was that it would happen again. Looking back, we were treating a longstanding mental issue without traditional medication and therapy, not knowing the cause of what it was. And at that time, maybe it did not matter. In those months I took the medications, I felt great. But it was not sustainable, and this is the problem with alternative therapies. I was spending at least an hour a day taking about 30 capsules, powders, and spending a mortgage payment doing it. And I made $37,000 a year.

The doctors who work outside of insurance, for both their care and the medications they give do this for one core reason. It's easier. Actually, it also may mean more money in their pockets – they can charge what they want and not worry about insurance companies giving them what is felt to be fair. But in their resistance to insurance companies and traditional methods, they also resist the people who need them. I remember a doctor I personally know saying to me one time that she had stopped taking insurance, because it "wasn't worth it." Well, my response was this: "Then you are only going to be helping one class of people."

Those who will always need the most help are those who cannot pay for it. Hence, needing the most help. In my final and worst episode of OCD to come, getting help meant stripping me of my financial stability. I would be newly divorced, my mortgage 50% of my income, and I was working full-time with a master's degree. If my disease had not been so bad that I was willing to give literally everything I had for treatment, I never would have gotten better. At one point, I quit my job just to rest, with no replacement job at hand. Today, I practice with the thought of what my clients are financially capable of at the forefront of consideration.

Eventually, I was stable, and I stopped taking the regiment while maintaining my stability. I still had chronic anxiety, and looking back, it mostly was present in my anger going forward. There was always that discomfort when I couldn't control something, and compulsive behaviors…over-talking, seeking reassurance, checking, and internally "responding" to my thoughts. But I was again, functioning as a seemingly normal person.

———————

There were many points in my first marriage I could have acknowledged that the relationship should not go on. But it wasn't until I turned 27, almost six years in, that it hit me hard in just the right way. And this time, in its final performance, I probably have OCD to thank.

Like everyone else's, our household only had one topic in the summer and fall of 2016: Donald Trump and Hillary Clinton. And like most social workers out there, my choice was predictable. My husband and I talked for months about it, seemingly on the same page. And then I blinked, and I saw my spouse drop a ballot in a box that very clearly read his vote as Donald Trump.

I flipped out. Despite all my antics that day, I legitimately felt my marriage was over. And in the realest sense there is, it was. This was the beginning of the end. I had known how different we were, our different lifestyles and priorities and dreams. But suddenly, our values were different as well. I did not know who I had married and felt I was living with a stranger. For months, I was in a fog. Many realizations happened during that time, and eventually, four months later, he came home and ended it. He knew I had checked out, he knew I couldn't go on, he knew we made each other incredibly unhappy, and on top of it all, he knew I wasn't heterosexual – something we had both known for years, but suddenly, he thought it the reason the relationship couldn't survive.

I hated politics. But to me, it's simply the caveat to bring out people's priorities, views, and values. Nobody will say all of what matters to them is on one side or the other, and I think most of us are more mixed than we want to admit. We don't want to admit we voted for this person, but disagreed with their views on homeland security, in favor of the opponent. But in the end, who won that election would take this country on two very different paths; thus, our future depended on it and the futures of the people I advocated for every day. To me, one value will always, always supersede the other: the right for us to be equal. The basic value of each human life, meaning the equity of all. Human rights. In my view, one side would choose to violate those rights while the other would work to protect them.

A poor relationship brings out the worst in both people. Good relationships make you better, they encourage you to be your best, do your best, and they see you at your best. My first marriage made us both worse. When I look back on the day we separated, I have nothing but utter gratitude for him. He did what I honestly couldn't. I was a strong person, but I had nothing left. I could not pull the plug. I'm not sure I would have, either. Even today, I don't think I could end a marriage – probably not a bad one, and surely not a good one. As hard as you try, if something is so opposed to who you are as a person, you cannot become it. Sometimes, it even disables actions that need to be made.

Marriage to me was eternal. It was the bond you choose and the struggles you don't, but at the end of the day, I wanted that bond. I just couldn't grasp that this was not it.

But older, wiser, and surely with less simmering mental health issues, he knew better, and he acted. And until today, it is the best thing anyone has ever done for me. It was my ultimate turning point to the life I was meant to live. If it wasn't for OCD, I would've lived it well at that point, but it wouldn't be until three years later that I was able to start doing that.

During this time, the inklings of obsession began, but they did not become full blown. Looking back, it was because there was no crisis of self, no decisions to make, nothing to consider. It just was. I felt an empty, deep void inside me throughout this time, and my mind was incredibly satisfied with the self-hate and shame I felt.

The only part of this experience that carried with me was the sudden, blunt, and unpredicted nature in which our marriage ended. It would leave me with this feeling that I could not foresee what would happen – specifically, who would leave, ever. It left me with a lack of felt stability that all people need, and certainly a lack of self-trust to know when something was coming - and something always was.

Someone once said to me that fate is what happens despite what we choose – that it will happen either way and is outside of our control. Of course, fate happens, but what we do with it is our choice.

When I was in my master's program years before, I had a professor who repeatedly told me that the university was starting a Doctor of Social Work program and that she thought I would be a perfect fit for it. I repeatedly stated I was done with that part of my life, but years later when the program began receiving applications and I qualified, I applied. This specific program – different from the PhD I had originally been in– was offered in less than ten schools in the country at the time. I had refrained due to the commitment to my marriage and the fear of my OCD. Now, one of those things could no longer keep me from it. I tepidly, subconsciously waited for the other.

The summer I got divorced, I began the program.

In that same month I began school, something even better came along, something OCD would enjoy destroying even more so than my program. The only thing that was perhaps more important.

That summer, I met my current wife. She was my person, the minute I saw her, and from the day we met, my world changed. I'll never see anything the same again.

When we met, she was planning to move away. I told her that I wanted her to stay. That I would move with her in three years, but that not everyone gets two chances at their doctorate. And that the degree was incredibly important to me. So, she stayed.

Those months renewed my love for life. Between a program I enjoyed, and finding Amanda, everything made sense again.

But I knew it was coming for this good thing in my life. Overtime, I felt it creeping into me. I would start to obsess, question, **doubt**. It wasn't a thought, or a feeling as much as a knowing that this thing would rip away my ability to be the person I needed to be for my job, for school, and for Amanda. I knew the episodes, and I knew when they happened – when life seemed to be working itself out in big ways. About 8 months into our relationship, one fight – our first fight – brought on the anxiety, and it Never. Stopped.

Fear

We all build internal sea walls to keep at bay the sadnesses of life and the often-overwhelming forces within our minds. In whatever way we do this—through love, work, family, faith, friends, denial, alcohol, drugs, or medication—we build these walls, stone by stone, over a lifetime. One of the most difficult problems is to construct these barriers of such a height and strength that one has a true harbor, a sanctuary away from crippling turmoil and pain, but yet low enough, and permeable enough, to let in fresh seawater that will fend off the inevitable inclination toward brackishness.

Kay Redfield Jamison, An Unquiet Mind: A Memoir of Moods and Madness

I was 21 years old the first time I stepped into a psychiatric unit. I was studying psychology, applying to PhD programs, and at that point, I had been learning about mental health for seven years. I was always drawn to those who were suffering emotionally, feeling capable of being a source of support, comfort, and solidarity.

As interested as I was, I hated being in the unit. It was a place of hopelessness, despair, primitiveness. It was dark, with the dim overhead lights littering the ceiling and a sense of misery felt throughout – not just when I was with the patients, but also with the employees. People didn't walk, they dragged. Nobody was living, they were just surviving.

I helped facilitate the recreational therapy groups. The unit was split into two sides, one for substance abuse and another for mental health. I felt like bait with the substance abuse patients. I was goggled at, taunted, and always on edge. I think it was then that I decided to never work in addictions.

I wish I could say working with the mental health patients was easier. Many of them had been through the unit dozens of times before. All seemed to have psychotic disorders, multiple suffering from schizophrenia. They would scream, push, throw chairs. And then, some were catatonic.

I will never forget one girl. About my age, a history of psychiatric admissions, diagnosed with schizophrenia and a bipolar disorder. She would stare at me for hours, her long, lanky body always standing near me. She never talked, and seemingly never even breathed. But she did perceive. She knew my walk, she knew my look, and at the time, it felt like she knew every thought, every memory I had ever had.

I was always glad to leave. The experience should have deterred me away from the field of mental health. The discomfort I felt should have pushed me in another direction. But I was perseverant and stubborn, and I felt an ability to understand minds suffering from mental illness. I persisted and entered my PhD program that year. But I vowed I would never step foot in another facility like this. Little did I know how things would look in eight years' time. Little did I know that one day, I would enter by choice. Not as the therapist, but as the patient.

———————————

Before my obsessions and anxiety would claim my sanity later that year, someone I knew encouraged me to attend a three-day seminar. I had come to an info session after someone who had helped me and who I respected tremendously encouraged me to. Always open for growth and learning, I signed up.

As I looked around on the first day of the seminar, I think that I saw something that the other 150 people or so in the room did not: broken people looking for salvation.

I pushed myself to be positive and to sit through the program anyways. After all, most similar programs looked like this from the outside looking in.

It started off light. We talked the entire first day about the fact that everyone in the room was *looking for* something. That we had suffered, that the world felt distant, and that we no longer wanted to feel the pain that we did. The entire first day was filled with descriptions of the emptiness "we all felt" and promises of transcendence.

The second day, people got up and began speaking to the group about what had happened to them in their lives. The parents of children who had been lost, the spouses of those who had cheated, and the victims of molesters who had robbed them of innocent childhoods. It was intended that we were shocked, that we were enthralled by the horrific stories before us. That we began thinking about our own traumas, allowing us to further connect to the other people in the room. As a therapist who had heard plenty of these stories in my time, the intended shock factor didn't quite hold me in the way that it did the rest. The other people seemed to be brainwashed by such trauma and hypnotized by the promises of forever happiness. A handful of people, like myself, were clearly not as entranced by the whole performance. But I stayed, as did they. I stayed in hopes that I was wrong and because it felt unsafe to admit I wasn't quite under the same trance that the others clearly were.

The epitome of the experience was when these victims began to stand at the front of the room and be drilled by the instructors. *Oh, he raped you? Are you sure that happened? What part did you hold in this experience? What responsibility do you have? Maybe you should stop hating him and call him and apologize. Are you sure it happened that way? And if it did, it was meant to happen. He was meant to rape you. Don't come back until you call him and forgive.*

And they ate it up. At first, they fought back. They argued and denied and cried. But they remained. They were emotionally abused and beaten into believing they were not victims, that this was simply a mentality they had chosen. That they had part in what had happened – everything that had happened - and it was their destiny. And finally, that they were glad it had happened. *Choose it,* they said. *Go back and choose that it happened. You are glad it happened.* And then, they were. They chose it. By the end of the second day, participants were laughing, dancing, and their smiles were glued.

I did not return the third and last day, but something had fractured inside my head. This experience today reminds me of the vulnerability of the obsessive mind. How easily it can be jolted. Of course, there were many in that room without my background who were not able to see it for what it was: abuse and manipulation to buy in to the other programs to come. There were *many* programs, which was not known at sign up – you only paid for this one to let them manipulate you into the rest. Because after all, if you didn't continue, you would be forever broken.

I left in tears and began having severe anxiety. While on surface, it hadn't gotten to me, perhaps some of those brainwashing tools had affected me as well. Possibly, I unconsciously believed that by me leaving, I was doomed to misery. This is when I remember my anxiety beginning in my final, undiagnosed episode of OCD.

———————

Amanda and I are a happy couple. Very happy, and very lucky. Both of us knew instantly that we were meant to find each other. The same amount of time I had been married, she had been single, and we always felt that she had somehow waited for me. We first met at a restaurant, and she would not stop staring at me as I spoke. I'll never forget how her smile radiated a kindness I hadn't felt in anyone before. We took everything slow, but our feelings were way ahead of us, and we didn't seem to have any control over that.

Amanda will always make me feel like I'm fortunate, despite my struggles. Sometimes, you find someone who makes it all make sense, and even the things that don't, you can let go of. Later, mentally ill and at my very worst, I would nearly sabotage our relationship. Today, I am grateful each day for my health, my strength, and my ability to live the life we both have planned together.

I had come out of a marriage of six years in which time I had lacked trust for various reasons. I felt I didn't know the person I shared a home with. When Amanda and I first had a conflict, it was regarding a lie she had told me. I was scared that I had been wrong about her. Honestly, my anxiety in response to my obsessive thoughts skewed the entire situation, and I became paranoid. While it seemed minor, it felt serious. I berated her for about a day before she broke up with me, and this moment changed the course of my health and our relationship.

We talked and made up, but she had just triggered two relationship wounds of mine. Drug use, and abandonment. And probably also the insecure feeling that I would always screw up relationships. Essentially, my lack of self-trust.

This was the first time that I had obsessed on this relationship, and this was where my OCD truly began its feast.

––––––––––––

OCD can take many forms. Hundreds, if not more. As a child, I obsessed mostly on numbers, losing control, and symmetry which gave way to compulsions to include stealing, touching and checking objects, my body, eating, counting, and reassurance seeking. In my final episode, it began with relationship obsessions.

Common Obsessions

Sexuality	Relationships	Scrupulosity	Numbers
Symmetry	Germs	Blurting Out	Sex

Relationship OCD is a kind of obsessiveness that feeds on intimate relationships. While it can deteriorate a relationship, it can also affect one's ability to function in other areas, as all kinds of OCD can.

Doubts in relationships are normal, and all relationships experience up-and-down feelings regarding one's partner. For those with this kind of OCD, however, the **doubt**ing is insufferable and can become increasingly time consuming and dysfunctional. My on-and-off symptoms of OCD over the years along with my recent history made for a perfect storm for relationship OCD.

If I could tell you how many times I googled "how do you know it is your person," it would probably be thousands.

Thousands. The relationship myths with which I grew up, and most of us believe, further twisted my perception of my relationship.

*If it's your person, there are never any **doubts**.* My mom said this often growing up, but I can tell you from my own experience with my parents, my parents have had plenty of their own **doubts** too. I now realize that people are deniers when it comes to their relationships – all partners say screwed up things at times, and part of commitment is loving them anyways. We will not always like the person we are with, and sometimes it even takes us a few days to realize 'oh, we do still love them, that's good.'

The right relationship should be easy. Really? Because I think that often the most important things are quite difficult.

You will feel complete when you find them. I felt happy when I found Amanda. Happy, less angry, more fulfilled. But only I can complete me. I still had anxiety, and actually, because good things actually made my OCD worse, it pulled me into my final full-blown obsessive episode. If I hadn't met her, I wouldn't have struggled, and then suffered, and then been treated. My love for her pushed me to be my best and give everything I had to my own recovery. But it did not make me better, in any sense.

Sometimes, relationship OCD feeds at the past. While my thoughts fed at my current relationship, they also began feeding at stories I had heard regarding Amanda's past relationships. I was a person who had never known jealousy, yet suddenly, I couldn't sleep due to it. I knew my obsessions made her feel ashamed and judged, as much as they made me feel jealous and out of control. But I couldn't stop.

This OCD can be focused on relationships or focused on specific partners. I have also heard it called retroactive jealousy – a form of jealousy that is often related to OCD and is about the person's past rather than present occurrences. I questioned both the relationship in general as well as my partner. I constantly checked how I was feeling about her and the relationship, I obsessed about her past, I focused on sex, I made comparisons, I asked for reassurances while also giving them to myself, and I talked about the relationship in therapy and to anyone else who would listen.

As I will talk about later, OCD can be vindictive. It knows the sufferer. It will feed at topics that are crucial to you. Motivated by the shame and guilt of my divorce and the decline of my first marriage, I had promised myself that I would be the kind of partner that I was proud of. My obsessions were furthered by the above myths I believed about relationships and my fear of choosing "wrong" again. I had no sense of trust for myself given the partners I had been blinded to in the past. I figured time would pass, I would commit, and I would one day find out that the person in front of me was not the person that I had thought. I didn't **doubt** her, I **doubt**ed my own instincts, vision, and judgment.

Ultimately, I feared loss. It was one thing that I had lost the wrong person, but I didn't feel strong enough to survive the loss of the right one. If I wasn't worried that I would somehow screw it up – by being confused about my sexuality, by losing control emotionally, by being verbally aggressive as I had been previously, by not seeing what was right in front of me - I was worried she would.

This fear of loss has fed much of my obsessions over the years. It has obsessed on my mistakes, impending tragedies, and my career. But after finding the girl who was truly my everything…it had its ultimate fun.

I had had symptoms of this disorder since my childhood in varying degrees. But after I went through a rough marriage and divorce at 27, at the same time I came out as "not straight" to others, it seemed I had all these brand-new insecurities that became a breeding ground for my obsessions. I was very much broken, and yet, I found the love of my life, Amanda, at this broken time. I can't know for sure, but perhaps only the love for her and our plans for the future would give OCD the footing it needed to push me to my lowest Bottom, while giving me the strength I needed to fight for my life.

When my head became out of control, I first hoped it was a repeat of the hormone imbalance I'd had years before, so it could be treated fast. But after months of hormones, my anxiety was still in full force. I went on Selective-Serotonin Reuptake Inhibitors (SSRIs) – laymen terms, antidepressants - for six months to no avail.

With the first medication I tried, Luvox, nothing happened. I felt no different. After about a month, I had a doctor friend who checked in with me and told me that I was on a "baby dose," and I should be taking at least four times as much as I was. My friend was furious that my doctor put me on the kind of dose a child would take. Being a friend, she could not treat me and lived elsewhere, so I talked to my doctor about the dosage, which she refused to raise.

I texted this friend dozens of times per day and given the tough time she was having in her own life, that would be the first friend I later realized I had overwhelmed with my obsessiveness. She stopped responding. From there, I went to a psychiatrist, who switched me to Lexapro.

The side effects were horrendous. I had a headache 24/7, nausea, and my anxiety only became worse. When you start taking medications, there may be side effects the first week or two, but those that don't go away may never, eliminating the medication as a possibility. This psychiatrist had diagnosed me with Generalized

Anxiety Disorder, and even though I admitted my obsessions and talked about the fact that I was picking at my skin unconsciously (an obsessive-compulsive disorder called excoriation), he didn't reconsider his diagnosis. After about a month, he still wanted me to remain on the medication and increased the dosage, despite the side effects. I ended up leaving, thinking that perhaps I had Premenstrual Dysphoric Disorder, and went to the only doctor who was consistent and knowledgeable about my care, the only doctor who really listened to me – my gynecologist.

She switched me to Prozac, and the same lack of effect took place with this medication as it had with the first. After about a month and one small increase in dosage, I didn't believe medication would work on me at all. I believed I officially had far too much **doubt** in medication altogether for it to work. I also had a therapist who did not really believe in medication. Instead of following the recommendation of my doctor, who wanted to increase the dosage, I gave up on meds and focused on therapy.

––––––––––––––

My therapist back then was someone I will never forget. She spent hours and hours of time during sessions with me. She loved me and wanted desperately to figure out what it was that was bothering me. I processed the trauma of the older, childhood friend, with the use of various techniques and therapies. Nothing worked. She stated to me once, *"what just doesn't make sense to me is this – you have handled the lows of your life with more than just grace…with humility, and with strength. But the highs – those you can't seem to handle…"*. And she was right. It only happened when things were good, and because of it, I had already unconsciously made sure that my life of the last decade was never all that good.

As Amanda and I's relationship grew – as we moved in together, travelled to Europe, got engaged – so did this thing inside me. It was this feeling that in trying to not destroy my relationship, I was choosing to destroy myself. I knew the good of the relationship could not last, and that little demon inside my head had been at work the entire time, feeding my overwhelming sense of **doubt**.

She would leave. "No, I won't Britt."

I would cheat. *But I've never even been tempted to cheat.*

Maybe I'm not gay. "Britt, you definitely are. Or whatever you want to call yourself - does it matter?*"*

Move that frame or something bad will happen. She will die. *Frame moved. And then moved again. And again.*

Sexual thought about another person. *Oh my god, am I turned on? I don't seem to be…but maybe I'm wrong.*

What if I commit and ruin another relationship? *There is a 50/50 chance! You probably will, you do ruin a lot of relationships…*

What if she doesn't really love me? *She clearly does.* But how could I know?

Can a relationship right after a divorce ever work? *Why did we meet so early? Is it doomed?*

Maybe I'll kill myself. *You would never do that! You aren't even depressed!*

Go back and lock the door. Someone will steal the car. It's not locked! *Late to an appointment to check the already locked door multiple times.*

I would seek reassurance obsessively from other people. That I wasn't going to cheat, that I was gay, that I was not doomed. If someone said something like *"There are no guarantees,"* I freaked out. I needed a guarantee. *I'm not getting better, I am getting worse.* But everyone else told me I was fine, so they reassured me repeatedly that that could not be true. Hearing I was fine would counteract the **doubt**ing I had that I was. I trusted other people more than I trusted myself.

Common Compulsions

Checking	Exercising	Touching	Counting
Praying	Reassurance Seeking	Washing	Ordering

I didn't just seek reassurance. I obsessively wrote in a journal. I took notes in my phone. I checked. I clicked. I pushed. I surfed the internet a minimum of 8 hours a day looking for answers about my thoughts, about my emotions, about *what was wrong with me.*

I did two rounds of Eye Movement Desensitization and Reprocessing (EMDR). I stuck with my therapist at that time for quite a while. She charged me with the consideration of what I was earning. Even though I agreed to pay her $70 per session, she only took $50, and she spent far longer than an hour with me per visit. Over time, I could sense her frustration with my lack of progress and even my continued deterioration, and it only fed my sense of low self-worth. I began to think about leaving her. I began to **doubt** my progress.

One day, after my therapist believed I had missed an appointment that I had cancelled a week before, she yelled at me. She said that she thought I had wanted help, that she didn't understand why I couldn't stick to the treatment plan, and that she just didn't know what to do with me. Despite my repeatedly telling her that I had cancelled the appointment via email, she stated that I had not. I was questioning the use of EMDR at that time, as I didn't believe I would be helped by it any further. We hung up, and a few days later, I wrote her an email saying I would no longer see her, and that her countertransference and resentment of charging me so little was seeping through to me, and it was not helping me. She wrote back expressing regret and stating that she was sorry for her outburst and that she truly cared for me.

I contacted a hypnotherapist following someone's recommendation – the therapist who would end up contributing heavily to my worsening of symptoms and then entrance into a hospital. She charged $215 a session, $165 if I paid up front, and acted like a high-priced scam. During our first call, she listened and then stated that she could help me, and I would be better and the "the best" after our sessions together.

By this time, I had stopped working as a social worker after being diagnosed with PTSD after my divorce. My anxiety and burn out had reached a tipping point, and I had quit suddenly, after nearly five years. I was working as a teacher, and the price of therapy was beyond my reach, but I had credit cards and she did state that hypnosis was "usually about 3 sessions." I could front three sessions.

In our first session, we spent the time reviewing what was happening for me. At the very end of it, she stated that to get the $165 rate, I had to pay for 10 sessions up front. She could not tell me how many sessions it would take (though she had alluded to 3 sessions total on the phone, and had already completed one session with me), but that ten would probably be enough. I was vulnerable, and as most people with severe OCD **doubt**s are, gullible and easily manipulated by words. I paid for the ten sessions, knowing I was quickly reaching the end of what I could handle. I was vulnerable and desperate.

She was very spiritual and said wacky things; she also believed that I was acting on instinct, that my thoughts were real, that perhaps Amanda and I should split. *Yeah, that'll work.* All I knew was the anxiety I felt was too much. It had become completely unbearable. Amanda and I were thinking about taking a break – my suggestion and supported by the therapist. After all, if I didn't give her up, it would swallow me. If I didn't act on the repulsive, hurtful thoughts I considered to be demands at that point, I would disappear.

Near the end of my ten sessions, I didn't feel much better. I had reached my end, had no strength left, couldn't pay for more sessions, and my partner and I were planning to separate. By this point, my partner thought I needed to go "sow my oats" and could not stick around for that. I knew that I didn't want to separate, didn't want to sow oats, but I also had no clue what I did need, except to make it stop. I needed the anxiety gone. I needed the thoughts to stop. And I would do anything to make that happen. As we planned to separate and as I responded to my obsessions by further considering various compulsions, it would ease a bit, but I didn't *want to* separate and do the things I thought my mind was pushing me to do. I just wanted all of it to stop.

By this point, I trusted my mind more than whatever part of me remained. I began to keep my thoughts to myself and compulse on my own. Internet, checking, writing. I found an article online about OCD, and I wanted to tell my therapist that I had figured out what was wrong with me. I always, always needed validation or I could not act – on everything. *No matter what she says, you know this is true. Hold strong!* I knew she would not believe me, somehow, as she hated labels. I knew she would fight me on it, because she had told me my thoughts were directing me in the "right" direction – she believed it too. And beyond anything, I knew my mind would fall into the **doubt**ing game again. By this time, I believed my thoughts were messages from God, a belief encouraged by this very therapist. All of her "you are having these thoughts for a reason" and "your mind is guiding you" talk had turned my moderate symptoms severe. To be fair, I don't think she realized that my beliefs were psychotic delusions. And nor did I.

When I told her that I thought I was experiencing OCD, it was then that she yelled at me. She told me to stop labeling myself, that nothing was wrong with me, and that everything that happened and was happening to me was meant to be. She referred me to my third and final psychiatrist but warned me that all the medications would permanently damage my brain. I made an appointment but had **doubt**s. I had tried meds. Nobody could help, and I was drowning.

This was on a Monday. I was taking anti-anxiety medication every morning just to get up and teach. By this point, OCD had taken my career, my health, and any positive feeling I had ever felt. After a non-therapist friend suggested that I had a dependent or borderline personality disorder, I had more **doubt**s, I was petrified, and I think I realized that I truly needed help.

On Thursday of that same week, I forgot to take the anti-anxiety medication. I sat at my desk at work, then got up, students filing into my room, and walked right out of my classroom. I drove myself to the hospital through 45 minutes of pouring rain, my family begging me not to go, and my therapist texting me that I was making a mistake and to stop trying to sabotage my life. I had a dream that night.

———————

I was driving in my car when the car began to slow down. The more I became angry and frustrated, the slower the car would go. Sometimes, it would completely stop. The people I love were around me, and I knew that they blamed me for it. They wouldn't stop talking. It was something about me that was allowing the car to stall, spit, and stop. But nobody else would, or could, drive for me. The more I took my eyes off the road, whether it be to look at the people around me or to listen to my own thoughts or the words being said, the worst it became. Finally, I realized what was going on. *The more I used my mind, the less I could use my feet - the less the car would work!* I learned this worked the other way as well.

The more I accepted and ignored my mind, the more I could use my feet.

Residual

The experience of obsessive-compulsive disorder is not typically loud. There are no screaming matches, no episodes of paranoia, no high moods, no chronic periods of suicidality. It creeps up on its victims, slowly takes hold of their minds. So slowly, that before many know it is happening, they are suffering - like a lobster in boiling water. There is little truth to its stereotypes, as it looks different across and within each instance. It leaves behind an unknown number of casualties who will never know what they could've been without it.

It is silent suffering.

Right alongside the days filled with powerless despair, it is amazing how much choice I had. Even when I was hanging on by the tips of my fingers, no control for what was going on inside or outside of me, I chose to hang on for a very long time. Eventually, my fingers gave up. All fingers do. They break, they cramp, they let go of the weight of your body. But any moment before that happens, you can choose to hang on or let go.

Letting go is not giving up, though. It is simply that - letting go. Letting the inevitable happen, knowing that perseverance can only delay, but not overcome.

I wish I had let go sooner. I wish my dutiful fingers had just slipped. But it was in my blood to fight. I was always a fighter, and one thing pushed me to keep fighting – hope.

Hope keeps us in denial. Hope leads us to thinking that help that just isn't coming will show its face. Hope, for me, led to my ultimate suffering. I didn't want to admit I was drowning. It had become so bad – the anxiety, the **doubt**ing, the rumination, the mental compulsions and nonmental ones – I just could not pretend one more day. I was now over-using my anti-anxiety medication (or as my later doctor would say, correctly using based on what I needed to function) I had been prescribed five years before for intermittent anxiety.

Relationships that attempted formation in that time failed. I made zero friends. I didn't have the energy to brush my hair, no less pretend I cared or even *heard* anything other people had to say.

I have a friend who once told me that after her daughter died, when she was at the funeral, someone waved at her, and that she just could not wave back. When you are at your bottom, there is nothing left. Not for a wave, not to eat an extra dessert, nothing. I had absolutely no energy beyond what I was already expending for mere survival.

My anxiety became so unbearable that every single minute that I was not in the presence of another, I crumbled. I hid the worst of it for years, on and off, from those who loved me. To them, I was a mess. I was anxious, insecure, determined to be unhappy.

The inherent **doubt**ing I had that something was wrong, hushed away by others who were convinced I was normal, was pushed down hundreds of thousands of times with reassurance from both others and myself. This became my main compulsion – getting reassurance.

Reassurance I was a good partner. That I could marry again and not screw everything up. For someone who wanted a happy relationship most, this was everything to me. My divorce and the subsequent shattered self-confidence led to my relationship **doubt**s. The lack of knowledge of my sexuality when I was young had furthered those **doubt**s. Did I know myself now? What if I was, again, wrong?

I was scared that I once again did not know myself, like before. And with this fear, I thought what most people think in that situation: I am not ready to settle down, not ready to embrace the happiness I had found. That I didn't know enough about myself, alone. And this thought is what haunted me for years. This thought was the final obsession of my untreated OCD, before I got real help, before I was diagnosed.

Some of my **doubt**s were trauma-induced, such as my fear of failing another relationship. Not just a relationship, but *the* relationship. With my person. Some of my **doubt**ing was a product of not fitting into a box. My sexuality **doubt**ing was a real insecurity it would take me years to overcome.

I cannot understand the belief that a person chooses who they love. I think that sexuality is viewed to be more simplistic than it actually is. It isn't about sex. In any situation, most people if not all people can be intimate with either sex. They can become aroused in the right context, and that context is only somewhat having to do with the sex of the person.

At the end of the day, sexuality is about who you can love. In my professional and personal experience, it is rare for a person who feels "very straight" or "very gay" to have had deeper feelings for someone of the sex not part of that identity. Even with effort to be in loving relationships with those people, it will never be the same. These are the people who must accept who they are, because even with the grandest of efforts, it is not going to change.

My sexuality is not extreme to one side or the other. I have loved both. Two men and two women, to be exact. However, my love for the two women was beyond that of the two men, so I label myself gay.

I struggled to label this for years, however, because I really don't fit neatly into the stereotype of 'gay.' I felt I didn't know who I was, but I knew I loved my female partner beyond anyone else, ever. Because of this confusion – a confusion that further contributed to a poor marriage and divorce – my sense of not being linear or "right" drove my obsessions wild.

As discussed, there are plenty of forms of obsessions in OCD. Over the years, I have experienced most of them to some degree. It's kind of like switching from one addiction to another, one outlet to another. One form of self-harm to another.

One of the forms of OCD I had, on top of the relationship and sexuality obsessions, is called "Just Right OCD." These obsessions are thoughts and/or feelings that something is not quite right or that it is incomplete. For example, you have a feeling that the cleaning of the stove is not quite complete, or that when using a door handle, your fingerprints are somehow smudged or sitting there on the handle and you must wipe it again. You may park your car multiple times or check emails more than is necessary to avoid any misses. Even when something is complete and seemingly perfect, you have this feeling that something is off. That there must be something askew.

I experienced these feelings that something was "off" or that I was somehow wrong in some unknown way in these final years. Usually, they pertained to my relationship and/or my sexuality. With something subjective and abstract, such as sexuality or love, individuals with this kind of OCD may never live without the feeling that they don't quite know everything they should, that they aren't quite sure enough. Rather than letting go of these unsure or incomplete feelings, those with just right OCD obsess on them, trying to alleviate or fix the things that aren't quite right.

These more abstract, intangible forms of OCD are more difficult to treat. The indicated treatment for OCD, Exposure and Response Prevention, includes a hierarchy of known triggers for the obsessions. But often, the triggers in this kind of OCD are endless and constantly accumulating. However, some ideas of possible triggers are categorized by the International OCD Foundation below:

o   Sight. Example: A person feels that his/her comb is not in 'quite the right place' on the dresser and might proceed to pick it up and put it back down – repeating until the feeling of incompleteness is gone.

o   Sound. Example: A person practicing piano feels that a certain note is 'off' and needs to play it over and over until it sounds right – even though tuning of the note has not changed in any real way.

o   Touch. Example: After touching a table, a person feels a sudden need to touch it again (and again) until a feeling of tension/distress goes away.

o   Personal Expression. Example: A person might need to express himself/herself 'precisely' in written or spoken words (even in his/her own head) – 'working through' wording until it meets their own standards of being 'just right.'

My past, my lack of self-trust, and my fear all clashed together hard and fast, and reached a boiling point. I couldn't turn the obsessions off. I either didn't have the strength or the knowledge to know what to do with the unnamed, misunderstood symptoms. The mild symptoms of OCD I had born for as long as I could remember became worse. And again, worse still when I began to believe the thoughts in my head were prophetic. That I was psychic, that this thinking was from God and every aspect of my mind that was inherently Brittany was the falsehood.

When I was diagnosed, despite the newfound knowledge of my illness, I had to have more trust in those first months than I've ever had in my life. I had to trust one more professional to not make me worse, yet again. To know what medication I needed, what I did not need, and to not miss something critical. I had to trust that one day, I would live moments without crippling anxiety and overpowering obsessions, even though I knew it would take a lot of time. I had to trust that my partner would accept "what" I was, that my parents would support my treatment, and thus not cause me more detrimental **doubt**, and that one day, I would even be happy. That one day, I would both know myself and love myself again. And I had to do all of this in the moments of my life when I was most vulnerable, and never more unlike myself.

––––––––––––

The hospital. A time I don't really talk about. Of course, I don't really desire to talk about it, but the main reason I don't is the looks on the faces of people when I do. Pain, empathy, anger. I know it causes pain to those who love me to remember that day.

Growing up in a family who doesn't talk about mental health, certainly doesn't go to therapy, and would prefer almost anything than be "dependent" on medication, my entrance into this dark place was probably one of the lowest days for the people who loved me, specifically, my partner and my parents. No part of them could understand, and a selfish part of me will always wish that they could.

My partner was filled with anger. In low moments, most of us are predictable. We become our worst selves, with the emotions that tend to come up first for each of us when having a hard time. I become anxious, my partner becomes irritated or angry. She was furious, as partners usually are when they disagree with your actions, are pushed away in bad moments, and are kept in the dark. She now realizes that her response was not fair, but she believed, as probably most people did, that it was some "choice" I had made without the help from her that she deserved the chance to give. I was yet another person in her life who had mental vulnerabilities and had ended up in a place so far gone that she was helpless to help. On top of that, her worst fear was failure, and this was, to her, the ultimate failure. She hadn't realized I was drowning.

My parents were filled with despair. They screamed, my mother threatened, and then she begged. She is the type to try to control when at her worst, and she did just that. Even inside the facility, she called throughout the day and even threatened the nurse who answered after I had gone to sleep that I "better be" alright.

I hadn't planned on telling my family where I was going. I had asked two of my closest friends, on the way to the hospital, to tell my family that evening so I wouldn't interrupt their workdays, and nobody could try to stop me. As friends usually do, they supported me. But one of these friends, thinking it was the right thing to do, contacted my family immediately.

A person chooses to go to an inpatient psychiatric unit when it has become very bad. It is a move you make out of strength, helplessness, and fear. It is, without a **doubt**, a *cry for help.* Those who check themselves in to these units are not being dramatic, they are being safe. They know they are at the end of a road, and they *do not know what else to do* and *where else to go.* And that was the clear line between those who protested, and those who supported. The fellow social workers, the medical staff, the teachers all knew I felt that I had to do it, that in my mind at that time, it was the only choice that I had. And they were correct. Even looking back, there is absolutely no other option I could have seen, no other choice I could have made.

I had thought about this move for a few days. I had asked my sister-in-law, who had been to this specific facility, about her experience. I had thought it was the only choice I had left. If I went anywhere else, they would ask for money up-front that I did not have. And my parents did not believe I needed help and would not have helped me until they realized it was this bad. So, this move also demonstrated to others that I was *not* alright, and regardless of their ability or refusal to accept this, it was the truth.

I signed myself in early in the morning, by 8am, with the promise that the doctor would see me that day. I waited and waited until I found out that the doctor had left for the day. At this point, my mother had begged me to leave, saying that she would get me in immediately to a psychiatrist and began calling doctors. But the facility would not let me out, even with proof that I was going directly to a psychiatrist. And even though they were denying me the doctor they had promised.

The system is completely backwards. I had signed myself in of my own accord, clearly stating I was not suicidal or homicidal, and yet, once I did that, only the doctor could decide I could leave. And this decision would not be made until I saw that said doctor, who apparently spent very little time with an entire unit of patients per day. I fought as hard as I had the strength to, saying I was a licensed therapist, saying I had mandated myself to be there, saying I had a doctor in the community who would take me *today* (unlike the facility's doctor) and sign off on it, but nothing worked, and I gave up. I could not fight, and I feared that if I did, I would only be held there longer.

Within suicide research, there is a theory called the suicidal mode:

> When the mode is activated, the person is cognitively and
> affectively restricted to suicidal thoughts and feelings of

hopelessness and helplessness. In most cases the suicide attempt leads to a reduction of inner tension and the deactivation of cognitive restriction—a cathartic effect. Afterwards, individuals often feel relief and again have access to life-oriented goals.

This mode, I believe, is something that relates to more than just suicide attempts. It is a mode that I have found in people who have even *considered* suicide, and it is a mode in which I believe I was in on this day. I had thought about the hospital for days, and I couldn't think of any other option but this one. Once I had made the decision I had been thinking about – though I didn't realize I had officially made the decision prior to making it – and once I was in the hospital, there was a kind of catharsis. Despite the brutal anxiety and despair, I felt before I checked in, after I got there, I felt peace. I finally felt that I was in a place where I didn't have to be surrounded by people who seemed normal. I didn't have to pretend that I also felt normal and that I was OK. I could let go. To this day, it was one of the most peaceful moments of my life, and I will never forget that feeling. I didn't feel happy or safe, but I did feel relief for the first time in 18 months. I felt like I had finally told the world the truth and couldn't pretend anymore – and I realized that the pretending and trying to hold it together was a lot of the battle. That feeling made me know that I was in the right place and had done the right thing.

People who have survived suicide attempts have described this mode; it is a pattern across these stories of survival. Once they have had this kind of release, they can again live. As if they were meant to attempt all along. As if part of themselves died in the attempt, and it was reborn into a part that wanted to live. After that day, I wanted to live too, in a way I hadn't felt in a long time. In letting go, I was able to regain the control I needed to survive my illness.

First thing the next morning, I saw the hospital psychiatrist. I insisted she listen to my story (I got 10-15 minutes out of her), and I was completely transparent about my symptoms. She told me, very confidently, that it seemed that I had severe depression. I was immediately helpless again, stating that I didn't know what was wrong, but that I did know what it wasn't – I was not suffering from Major Depressive Disorder. She stated, "you look pretty depressed to me," and I stated that I was being held against my will in a psychiatric unit, so yes, I was depressed, but that was the easiest diagnosis she could give, and I had not been depressed longer than a day. She wanted to prescribe medication, and I refused to take medication without a full evaluation. I promised that I had a psychiatry appointment the next day and would be in this doctor's care. With this, the hospital doctor signed my discharge papers, and I waited to be released.

Feeling shame regarding telling a stranger the kind of thoughts I was having, I went alone to the doctor. We met for an hour, but within the first ten minutes, the psychiatrist had my diagnoses. I was diagnosed with OCD, panic disorder, and said in a way that I will never forget, the "worst generalized anxiety disorder I have ever seen." Prior to putting me on medication, however, he wanted to be completely sure there wasn't anything else going on, as he said that I also seemed like a woman going through postpartum depression. I was referred to get a full hormone panel, given my history of hormone imbalance, and he swabbed my mouth for a test that would examine my DNA to see which SSRIs would metabolize correctly in my brain – not a foolproof test, but a good starting point, he said, for a patient who had no improvement on three different SSRIs (though we did acknowledge that the dosages had been far too low).

My hormone panel was clear, but the endocrinologist described to me a handful of patients he had seen over the years who "looked like" me. Highly anxious, no relief found, and with symptoms that mimicked a severe chemical imbalance. He stated that hormones were tricky, and even with perfect results, it wouldn't necessarily mean that I didn't have an imbalance. But that these patients would always come back to him years later, seemingly a very different person from the fragile ones he had first met. When I asked what kind of medication would allow someone like me to live with such symptoms, he said the same as the psychiatrist: very high dosages of SSRIs.

Two weeks later, with a clear hormone panel and a DNA test demonstrating that only 4 of the 42 SSRIs on the list would metabolize as they should in my brain, I began medication. Further, I was introduced to a genetic mutation called MTHFR, which was confirmed that I had. He stated that variants of the gene were common, but some people with it suffer serious side effects of the body not being able to metabolize folate, which our bodies need. Symptoms of this mutation could include: cardiovascular disease, depression, anxiety, bipolar disorder, schizophrenia, colon cancer, acute leukemia, chronic pain and fatigue, nerve pain, migraines, and recurrent miscarriages in women of child-bearing age. To this day, I take a folinic acid that provides my body a form of folate it can process, thus combating possible side effects of the mutation.

The first days of recovery, I focused on small things. At first, eating and taking medication and getting out of bed in the morning. I did not allow myself to stray from that regiment one bit, and after the first few days, I went to work.

I took my medication incredibly seriously. Unfortunately, it was all I had. In that time, I still had my highly expensive, unsupportive therapist, and it would be months before I truly realized how harmful she had been to me. I had myself, and my medication. I did not drink, smoke, and I took it exactly every evening, manipulating the time until I found what hour of day was best. I coped with some intense nausea the first few weeks. I left the toxic school I worked in and began a job in an elementary school that provided me the space and calm I needed to heal. I dealt with as little stress as possible those first few months, on principle, except for the one thing I could not set aside: my doctorate degree. And little by little, I improved.

I was very honest with the people in my life about my diagnosis. I felt that I wanted to be upfront about the reason behind my behaviors. I needed this, and I needed to own that I had not been myself for a long, long time. This truth, however, seemed to be far too much for some.

At the time, I didn't trust my own perceptions, but looking back, there are individuals who never saw me the same after I was diagnosed. Either because of the diagnosis itself being some sort of scarlet letter on my chest – *especially* to those who were counselors as I was, believe it or not – or because I was very raw during that time, and they did not give me the leniency and understanding that loved ones should. Perhaps I was oblivious, tired, emaciated, and unaware of my tone or words. I would be lying to say that the road to recovery felt anything but lonely and isolating. Coming back into the world your mind left long ago is painful. It looks and feels different, and even harder, *you* feel different, about yourself and about the world. And now, you must look at who you had become.

One of the main things I began to feel the effect of is how my illness had affected my family. Every day, every move, every choice you make causes ripples, and even though people want to forget and the ones who truly love you will let those things go, there are things that change.

There was a lot of whispered phone calls between my mom and family members, comments that I was gaining pounds back that I had not realized I had lost, alone time to process things I had said, as well as misunderstandings where I spoke before thinking or was perceived in a way that was unintended, damage already done. I was healing, and as I now acknowledge, I am a very slow healer, in every way. I had to reconcile the person I had become, what it meant for the person I was now, and what to do to become the person I wanted to be.

And then, there's time. Time is the one thing that once lost, you can never retrieve. I didn't miss days or months; I had missed *years* of my life while I was just existing. I will never forget that about three months after treatment, I recognized for the first time just how bright and vivid the colors red-yellow-green of the streetlights were. I was sure that at some point in the past, I had known these colors, but if so, I could not remember when.

I began to read the OCD manual that my psychiatrist had recommended to me. This book provided me all the education, skills, and thinking mechanisms I needed to understand and begin my recovery. It became my bible. Having the form of OCD they call "Pure O," my compulsions were mostly in my head, and everything in society was a trigger. This is a world made for the illicit, and not for people like me. I isolated, and years later, I still do. Not because I get anxious as I did, but because I am happier and more comfortable without those triggers and unpredictable distress at times.

I had words and behaviors and values I had to live by in the first year of my recovery, and they saved my life. Those with OCD can't just do whatever their mind or body or emotions want them to do, just like those with addiction don't get to follow their compulsive behaviors either. Our lives depend on us living by *who we are* rather than *what we think or feel.* There is no gray, there is only black and white. We must constantly skate between the fine line of compulsions and obsessions, and our true feelings, thoughts, and choices, after we first are able to realize what those distinctions are. The ironic thing is, while we have to give up our goals of certainty and control, we have to be very controlling and live very deliberately in order to also heal.

Early in my recovery, I had the constant feeling that it would be so easy to accidentally or quickly compulse and mess up in a big way. I feared mistakes, I feared being out of control. Mistakes felt so close, so possible. But then I would blink and realize that in reality, I was just sitting on a bench on a playground. That I wasn't in real danger of doing this thing that my mind was convincing me was imminent and likely. That every move I would make to do this thing is completely unlike me. I feared screwing up so badly that I had literally triggered full-blown obsessive-compulsive disorder. Every harm, every possibility felt imminent.

I stared at my nine-year-old students on the playground and wondered which of these kids would struggle the most? I could point out some who I could predict would struggle, but there are always the surprises. The one that doesn't show outward signs. The one like me. What would I have done if I had known I would be the one in my group of friends, the one in my family who would combat sexuality, divorce, and a severe mental disorder within three years of each other? Some days, it makes me feel like an outcast. Most days, actually. Others, it makes me feel like a survivor. But either way, it's invisible. There's no disability sticker, no scarlet A, no cast. But it is a disability, I am an outcast, and it does hurt.

The thing that I am always surprised about, looking back to the multiple times in my life that OCD hit me hard, is how functional I was. Other people had to do more than just glance at me to take in that something was wrong. Actually, I could hardly convince someone that I was not OK. But as I improved, they seemed to be struck by how much I had truly been suffering. Health deteriorates slowly with mental illness, but once you find a center, it can improve fast. I gained weight, seemed more confident in myself (as I wasn't asking for reassurances from everyone), could look at people when speaking to them, and was able to really listen to others again. I was able to respect and defend myself where I needed to rather than falling apart when someone crossed a boundary. Prior to these changes, not even I knew how sick I had been.

Highly functioning people are survivors. Even at our worst, we will sleep and eat just enough to get by, go to work, pay our mortgages, and answer the phone. We do the big tasks, because it keeps us alive. We know priorities. It's the small things that change. The lack of 8-hour sleeps, the deep breaths, the extra or lost weight, the small mistakes and lack of detail-orientation. When I was suffering from a severe depression at 25, I forgot how to spell my last name one time. I hadn't been born with the name, so perhaps it wasn't inherent in the same way that my first name was, but it had been my name for years. I sat there for a minute or two, trying to remember. And then, I wrote it down, and went back to work. Mental health can affect literally *everything*.

In those first days of recovery, I did not know what would happen. I didn't know if the medication would work, if my family would ever see me the same again, and if I was going to get better. But I did know one thing, and I used it to push through the days: my diagnosis.

I did all the research I possibly could. I learned everything there was to know about obsessive-compulsive disorder. If I was going to beat it, I had to know my enemy. And even if it meant years of training my mind, with no improvement from any other means, I was going to give it my all. Knowledge truly is power, and I finally had the knowledge I had been searching for to starve my monster.

There were days I banged my head against the walls, days I went to sleep at 7pm or didn't sleep at all. Days I threw up everything I ingested, and days I couldn't eat one single thing. Days I screamed, and in those first months, I was terrified of my thoughts never leaving. That if I didn't act on them, they would never go.

But with growing knowledge and encouragement from my psychiatrist, I learned that my compulsions had absolutely no guarantee of settling the obsessions. Actually, completing compulsions *made sure* the obsessions would never leave. Never. And I had my entire life as proof.

I lived with the assumption that my thoughts would never leave. I fought to get help, and then my help was this: medication, and accepting that this may always be hard. I realized that to survive and overcome my disease, I would have to be stronger than the thoughts themselves. That meant training my mind beyond anything I could have ever imagined. Controlling our minds was one thing, but I had to *ignore* and *accept* mine at the same time. This process would take me the better part of two years to master.

For those with OCD like mine, the need to be perfect is real. It's not a desire or a compulsion. It's a need. If we want to hold on to every little thing that matters to us, from our careers to the people in our lives, we absolutely must trust ourselves to not give in to what is, on some bad days, the greatest impulse that we have. It's like having an addiction and knowing that if you relapse, it better just be a few sips from that bottle, but not enough to become drunk. Because if you do, you cannot predict what you will do to or with all those things that you hold dear. Even if just one time. It only takes once.

But alcoholics can avoid having alcohol in their house. Or go another route to avoid the bad side of town and people they would associate with. OCDers whose illness is anything like mine cannot avoid the triggers, in many cases. Because it is all inside of our own heads.

————————————

I was supposed to meet with my doctoral research committee the August evening that I went into the hospital, so it was delayed. I had been done with my research project since the spring, and after waiting six more months to defend my research, it had to wait longer.

In November, three months after my hospital admission, I defended my doctoral research, having come a long way from my previous brokenness. In the days leading up to my defense, I was at the highest stress point I had felt since I was diagnosed. I worked full days, then every evening after work and on weekends, I would sit in my empty classroom on top of a desk, memorizing the 30 PowerPoint slides and the longer list of notes that went with them. Despite all I went through, this degree was the only thing that I had not allowed myself to risk. My relationship, my family, my money, and my career, all damaged. But not this degree. I felt that if I did not do this right – *just right* – none of it would have been worth it. I would crumble. And on top of that, I felt it may push me to relapse.

Relapse. Something, as my psychiatrist would say, everyone does. I still am unsure what relapse looks like, thankfully, but I do know that I spend every day of my life preventing it. And I do know that I have promised myself that no matter how bad it gets again, it will not look like before. I will not consider forcing myself to do things against my own will and self to satisfy a demon inside my head.

I was stressed, scared, but I persevered, successfully completing my doctoral research defense.

That fall, I applied for professor positions around the country. Fresh out of the hospital, I received encouragement from my mom to apply to places "you and Amanda may want to live." Feeling tired, ill, and only beginning to get treatment, I applied because it was the only road I saw and the road that had been planned. I didn't know what I wanted, because I didn't even know who I was in those early days. I didn't know if Amanda would forgive me and choose to live a life where she had to trust I would always be stronger than my illness. But for about five months, I applied to about 100 jobs across the country, in anticipation of the degree I would earn the following spring. This was the only thing I did in planning for the future, and it was more out of duty and commitment than desire. The rest of my days were made up of talking myself into having faith that my obsessions would ease and encouraging myself to fight them off while lacking a response I had always used to cope with the distress from them – compulsion.

I made some promises to myself. I would not talk about the thoughts. My main compulsions had been reassurance-seeking and googling. I cut them both out completely a few weeks after I was diagnosed. I didn't say one word about them in fear of feeding the monster, not even to my therapist, and it was the very hardest thing I have ever done. A year later, I would still be fighting the urge to fulfill them.

That perseverance gave me one thing that made it easier.

It gave me my power back.

Educate

When I get in touch with the most intimate, painful, or confusing moments of my life, I often found myself faced with a choice: I could either focus on reliving old scenes in my mind's eye and let myself feel what I had felt back then, or I could tell my analyst logically and coherently what had transpired. When I chose the latter, I would quickly lose touch with myself and start to focus on his opinion of what I was telling him. The slightest hint of doubt or judgment would shut me down, and I would shift my attention to regaining his approval.

Bessel Van der Kolk in "The Body Keeps the Score"

I was sitting in front of my fourth psychiatrist when I was finally diagnosed. I knew, deeply, that his words were true, even though the truth had become so lost amongst the lies in my head. I knew because I had read the earlier-mentioned article about OCD, though I was deterred from believing it after my therapist had told me to "stop" trying to diagnose. But when I heard someone else finally say it – so casual, so firm, and yet so sure, I knew it was true. The truest thing I had heard in years. I hadn't been wrong; my therapist had been wrong. And her error had cost me.

Obsessive-compulsive disorder, like many other mental illnesses, takes lives, breaks families, and erases identities. It is isolating. The loneliness is real and crushing. But the most isolating factor is the misunderstanding from society, family, and friends, and even those practitioners who should know its presentation. OCD is not cleanliness. OCD is not arranging things, and it is certainly **not** perfectionism. It is not a disorder that anyone who knows its true nature would joke about. It is pain. It is a disorder in which the obsessions of the mind take over to a degree that controls your thoughts, emotions, behaviors, and eventually, your life.

The previous version of the Diagnostic and Statistical Manual of Mental Disorders, the DSM-IV-TR, included obsessive-compulsive disorder under the Anxiety Disorders classification. Despite anxiety being inherent to OCD, obsessive-compulsive disorder has its own unique presentation and prognosis. While 76% of those with OCD also have the diagnosis of another anxiety disorder, these disorders differ in comorbidity, prevalence, treatment, cognition, and emotion. Anxiety disorders do not include the presence of compulsions. In the current version of the DSM, due to the major differences between OCD disorders and other types of anxiety, OCD is in its own classification: obsessive-compulsive disorders.

The diagnosis of obsessive-compulsive disorder requires the presence of:

o   Obsessions (recurrent and persistent thoughts, urges, or impulses that are experienced, at sometime during the disturbance, as intrusive and unwanted, and that in most individuals cause marked anxiety or distress) that an individual attempts to ignore or suppress; and/or

o   Compulsions (repetitive behaviors - e.g., hand washing, ordering, checking or mental acts such as praying, counting, repeating words silently) that the individual feels driven to perform in response to an obsession or according to rules that must be applied rigidly.

The obsessions and compulsions are time-consuming and take at least one hour per day, significantly impairing the day-to-day life of the sufferer. This DSM-V was published in 2013, prior to the 2022 updates in the DSM-V-TR, and since then, we now know that OCD always has the presence of *both* obsessions and compulsions, not either/or. The compulsions of some individuals are simply invisible as they reside inside the minds of the individuals.

Obsessive-compulsive disorder affects 2-3 percent of the population and is one of the most disabling disabilities in our world due to the loss of income and quality of life. Despite its critical nature, it remains a highly misdiagnosed illness. The fact that OCD can present in many ways further gives way to this misdiagnosis. In lieu, the inability to correctly diagnose gives way to sufferers having distrust for medical professionals.

One study looking at the misdiagnosis rates of practitioners founded that while some varieties of OCD (symmetry and contamination obsessions/compulsions) were diagnosed accurately, other varieties (aggression, pedophilia, homosexuality, fear of blurting out inappropriate things, taboo thought OCD) were more often misdiagnosed. The first study by these researchers assessed primary care physicians' abilities to diagnose OCD accurately – as they are usually the first stop for sufferers; in another study later, they further assessed the rate at which mental health practitioners accurately diagnose OCD. Mental health specialists, with a 38% misdiagnosis rate, had only somewhat of a better understanding of OCD compared to primary care doctors (50% misdiagnosis rate).

Two years later, other researchers used the same vignettes as in these studies to see the rate at which the general population could identify OCD presentations. On average, half of the time, there was misdiagnosis – no better or worse than the misdiagnosis rate of professionals. In all three studies, "taboo thought" or Pure O OCD was the most highly misdiagnosed form of OCD. Consequently, most sufferers go undiagnosed for over a decade - even once professional help is sought, it is on average another two years before diagnosis is made.

In OCD, there are three levels of severity: 1. good or fair insight; 2. poor insight; and 3. absent insight. When someone with OCD has "good or fair insight," this person realizes that the thoughts and beliefs are *probably or definitely not true.* On the other hand, those with poor insight *think the thoughts/beliefs are probably true* while those with absent insight are essentially delusional in that he or she *are completely convinced the thoughts/beliefs are true.*

Many individuals with obsessive-compulsive disorder (OCD) have dysfunctional beliefs. These beliefs can include an inflated sense of responsibility and the tendency to overestimate threat; perfectionism and intolerance of uncertainty; and over-importance of thoughts (e.g., believing that having a forbidden thought is as bad as acting on it) and the need to control thoughts.

Individuals with OCD vary in the degree of insight they have about the accuracy of the beliefs that underlie their obsessive-compulsive symptoms. Many individuals have *good or fair insight* (e.g., the individual knows that the house is not more likely to burn down if the stove is not checked 30 times). Some have poor insight (e.g., the individual believes that the house will probably burn down if the stove is not checked 30 times), and a few (4% or less) have absent insight/delusional beliefs (e.g., the individual is convinced that the house will burn down if the stove is not checked 30 times). Insight can vary within an individual over the course of the illness. Poorer insight has been linked to worse long-term outcomes.

By the end of my crisis, I had no insight. I believed my thoughts had meaning – even the worst of them. Further, I believed I had to take action in response to the thoughts, or they would not leave. I believed the thoughts were me – that I had become the thoughts. That they were messages and most dangerously, that they had meaning and direction. I would perseverate between how insane these impulses were and believing them, the perseveration a product of not only my own mind, but who I was talking to about them. At the end, my therapist was the one who encouraged and supported my acting out compulsions. The back-and-forth diminished, and in thinking that I had to act on my thoughts –thoughts that disgusted and tortured me - I crashed. It was then that I went to the hospital.

Even though few OCDers have psychotic features, this does bring up a rule to recovery we must all live by: we cannot trust our own feelings because no matter what, knowing the difference between intuition and OCD is an art never totally mastered.

While some professionals will under-diagnosis us with anxiety or depression, causing lack of proper treatment and likely a progression of symptoms, others will over-diagnose, possibly causing a quicker and uglier progression of those symptoms. In such cases, practitioners have been known to misdiagnose those with OCD with psychotic disorders. In one case study, a boy misdiagnosed with the lifelong, psychotic schizoaffective disorder was medicated with anti-psychotics which led to a worsening of as well as new obsessive-compulsive symptoms. Those professionals who misdiagnose OCD are six times as likely to prescribe anti-psychotics – sometimes a dangerous choice for those who have OCD. Much suffering can result from this misdiagnosing. In two different case studies, the patients improved significantly after being taken off anti-psychotics, being diagnosed accurately, and beginning treatment for OCD instead.

Psychotic disorders feature hallucinations and delusions as their hallmark symptoms. OCD's hallmark symptoms are obsessions and compulsions. While severe OCD can feature psychotic features, these are caused by obsessions rather than being stand-alone, primary symptoms.

When people think of OCD, or joke that they are "so OCD," they mean one of a few things. They are clean, they are picky, they want things a certain way. They are essentially perfectionistic.

This is not OCD. Most of us with OCD are not super clean or super hygienic, and you probably cannot even tell that we have OCD. Though some people with OCD have obsessions about cleanliness, health, and symmetry that would present with associated compulsions, this is not the most typical presentation of OCD.

These stereotypes are closer to the actual presentation of obsessive-compulsive personality disorder. In one of the above studies, mental health practitioners confused presentations of OCD with OCPD 80% of the time. Per the DSM-V, OCPD is "a pervasive pattern of preoccupation with orderliness, perfectionism, and mental and interpersonal control, at the expense of flexibility, openness, and efficiency." It involves four or more of the following symptoms:

o   Preoccupation with details, rules, lists, order, organization, or schedules to the extent that the major point of the activity is lost o Perfectionism that interferes with task completion

o   Excessive devotion to work and productivity to the exclusion of leisure activities and friendships

o   Overconscientious, scrupulous, and inflexible about matters of morality, ethics, or values

o   Unable to discard worn-out or worthless objects even when they have no sentimental value

o   Reluctant to delegate tasks or to work with others unless they submit to exactly his or her way of doing things

o   Miserly spending style toward both self and others; money is viewed as something to be hoarded for future catastrophes

o   Rigidity and stubbornness

Personality disorders cannot be medicated away. The disorders themselves are part of the essence of the person. In definition, they are "an enduring pattern of inner experience and behavior that deviates markedly from the expectations of the culture, in terms of (2 of the following): cognition, affectivity, interpersonal functioning, and impulse control."

Because the obsessions of those with OCD are so anxiety-provoking, we try to get rid of them in any way we can, leading to compulsive behavior. The compulsions may make us feel better in the short-term, so we continue them, but the obsessions always return.

In the 19th Century, OCD was dubbed "The **Doubt**ing Disease." At first glance, that name doesn't fit, but with a deeper understanding of the nature of OCD, it is a perfect name to what is happening in every OCD sufferer's mind.

Those with OCD cannot tolerate **doubt**. A thought just like any other thought comes into our head. The thought is distasteful, negative, unpleasant. It may be a thought of putting a cat in a microwave. It may be a thought of touching a child's genitals. Having sex with the non-preferred sex. Or cheating. Blurting out something in appropriate.

We all have these thoughts. *All of us.* In fact, a large study of 777 university students across 13 countries demonstrated this finding in 2014. But the differences between those who have OCD and those who do not is not the thought content. It is the reaction. OCD is very much a thought disorder – over time, these thoughts "stick" in a way that they do not in other brains, and we emotionally respond to these stuck thoughts. Therefore, more than a thought disorder, it is an emotional one.

Those with OCD begin to over-analyze and over-consider the thought that comes. *What does it mean? Does this mean I am a pedophile? Or I am going to harm my child? Or my cat? Can I*

trust myself to not shout profanities in inappropriate situations?
Am I gay/straight? Is this the right relationship? Did I leave the
oven on? Am I possessed? Did I get HIV from that handshake?

The mind is random. Our thoughts are not us, and they
don't have real meaning, but they do know us. They can have a
plan of their own. They know our passions, our weaknesses. *Our*
minds know what matters to us.
Even worse, our minds go exactly where it hits the hardest:

o Religious? Obsessions of possession. Or screaming out in
   church.
o Relationship? Relationship **doubt**ing.
o Chaste? Loyal? Asexual? Cheating or sexual obsessions.
o Health or hygiene-focused? HIV or contamination OCD.
o Your children are your whole world? Obsessions about
   abusing or harming them.
o Love animals? Obsessing about hurting them.
o Consider yourself *very straight?* Obsessions about being
   gay.

And now you think this – given that the thoughts are so
opposed to what you really are, why would you think it? Unless
you aren't what you really think you are. Unless you only *thought*

you knew yourself. Maybe you are someone else entirely. Maybe the thought is the real you.

The anxiety becomes overwhelming and possibly completely unfunctional. You begin to convince yourself over and over again that you couldn't do what you fear. *Compulsion.* You get relief from the anxiety, and you keep on going.

You ask reassurance of others that you couldn't possibly do that. *Compulsion.* You get relief and keep on going. You keep taking showers [*compulsion*]. Keep on going.

The more you respond to the thoughts, the more you believe they have meaning.

These thoughts continue, and the **doubt**ing in response to these thoughts continues. And here the disorder begins. The **doubt** that the thoughts cause – the **doubt** in ourselves, in the future, in what will happen – tortures us. Some people even begin to question their very existence. OCD is nothing short of a dark, sinister, seemingly purposeful demon that knows your mind and more importantly, your heart.

The vicious cycle is caused by inherent **doubt**:

OCD can make a sufferer **doubt** even the most basic things about themselves, others, or the world they live in. I have seen patients **doubt** their sexuality, their sanity, their perceptions, whether or not they are responsible for the

112

safety of total strangers, the likelihood that they will become murderers, etc. I have even seen patients have **doubt**s about whether they were actually alive or not. **Doubt** is one of the more maddening qualities of OCD. It can override even the keenest intelligence. It is a **doubt** that cannot be quenched. It is **doubt** raised to the highest power. It is what causes sufferers to check things hundreds of times, or to ask endless questions of themselves or others. Even when an answer is found, it may only stick for several minutes, only to slip away as if it was never there. Only when sufferers recognize the futility of trying to resolve this **doubt**, can they begin to make progress.

The guilt is another excruciating part of the disorder. It is rather easy to make people with OCD feel guilty about most anything, as many of them already have a surplus of it. They often feel responsible for things that no one would ever take upon themselves.

Intrusive thought OCD – commonly known by the misnomer "Pure O" - is the most severe form of the disorder, both before and after treatment. It is also the most commonly misdiagnosed. The above case study that described the misdiagnosis of a teenage boy with a psychotic disorder also explained that it was an "unusual" case of OCD due to the fact that the intrusive thoughts led to actions. While most people with taboo intrusive thoughts do not act on those thoughts, some individuals who have no insight into the thoughts can believe those thoughts have meaning and respond to them as commands in order to rid of the thoughts.

The name "Pure O" was originally dubbed due to the belief that it consisted of only obsessions. However, it is now known to be a misnomer as it does also include compulsions. The compulsions are not seen since they take place inside one's head; common compulsions here include counting, praying, talking back to thoughts, or "checking" if they are having a sexual urge. These unwanted thoughts are often violent or sexual, causing severe anxiety that the sufferer will act on the thought. As it is largely misdiagnosed, practitioners often mistake these individuals as violent, pedophilic, or as various other damaging labels. Thus, the difference between someone with OCD and someone who is violent or sexual is important: the person with OCD is repulsed by the thoughts, and there is no real *desire* to act on them. Instead, there is fear that they will.

———————————

There are five diagnoses in the obsessive-compulsive disorders section of the DSM-V. Trichotillomania (hair-pulling) and excoriation (skin-picking) are included as they are compulsive in nature. Unlike OCD, however, there is not a required obsessive component to these illnesses. Most of the time, boredom is the cause of such behaviors. Early in my own final episode, I picked my skin consistently and unconsciously, often discovering the lesions later, but I was not diagnosed despite my report of this behavior.

Hoarding – excessive collecting of and difficulty getting rid of possessions – and body dysmorphia are also included. Body dysmorphia includes the "preoccupation with one or more perceived defects or flaws in physical appearance that are not observable or appear slight to others." At some point, the person has performed repeated behaviors or mental acts in response to the preoccupation (mirror checking, reassurance seeking, grooming). While body dysmorphia and OCD can be confused, body dysmorphic obsessions and compulsions are focused specifically on *appearance,* rather than perfection, symmetry, or other OCD-specific topics.

The Cycle of OCD

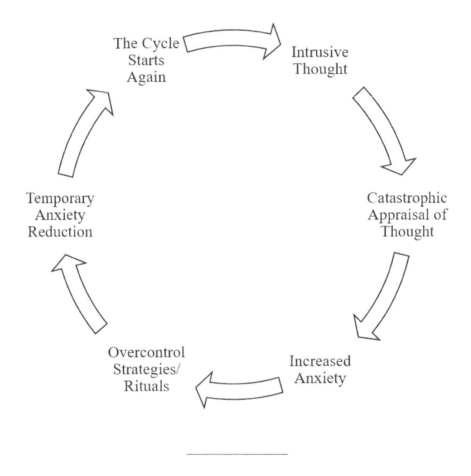

The Cycle Starts Again → Intrusive Thought

Intrusive Thought → Catastrophic Appraisal of Thought

Catastrophic Appraisal of Thought → Increased Anxiety

Increased Anxiety → Overcontrol Strategies/ Rituals

Overcontrol Strategies/ Rituals → Temporary Anxiety Reduction

Temporary Anxiety Reduction → The Cycle Starts Again

Obsessive-compulsive disorder is one of the few mental health diagnoses that has been found to have very real brain differences. There is difficulty in those with OCD recognizing "errors" in thinking and moving on from those errors without acting on them. In essence, the brain's thoughts easily ***stick.***

PET scans of OCD brains reveal a brain that does not rest. Activity levels in certain parts of the brain, including the limbic system - the emotional center of the brain - are much higher than in comparison subjects. Further, fMRI scans show the same activity differences. On the other hand, in certain areas of the frontal cortex, responsible for our highest cognitive functioning, those brains with OCD show less activity.

Similarly, in a study with 1700 participants in Amsterdam, major differences in the structure of OCD brains were found. In particular, they noted that the parietal lobe—a part of the brain thought to be involved in attention, planning, and response inhibition—was thinner in people with the disorder. These brain functions are often impaired in people with OCD, and such abnormalities can contribute to patients' uncontrolled repetitive behaviors.

For all sufferers, accurate diagnosis is important. Without knowing what we face and without educating ourselves to our own minds, we leave ourselves vulnerable to those minds. Minds that will always be present, in every bad or good thing that happens. Minds that are looking for vulnerabilities, flaws, opportunities to **doubt,** and traumas to feed from. We must be ready for this part of us to grow stronger at any time. Because in many cases, it will.

OCD has a more specified treatment regimen than other anxiety disorders. Treatment involves specified modals, such as Exposure and Response Prevention (ERP) therapy. ERP involves making a hierarchy of the triggers that exist for a person – those things that lead to obsessions and compulsions – and slowly exposing oneself to those things, in order, and repeating this practice until that thing no longer results in anxiety.

Someone with sexual obsessions may make a hierarchy that begins with a small trigger such as someone talking about sex. Higher up on the hierarchy could be seeing people have sex on television or thinking about their partner's past. The hierarchy is aimed at reducing the anxiety that every day triggers may bring by exposing us to those things, and thus learning to accept our obsessions without responding with compulsive behaviors.

Everyone with OCD, in order to recover, must accept a central notion: we cannot prevent, reduce, or control our thoughts. We may never have a reduction in our obsessions, and to some degree, they will always be there. The goal of treatment is to live with them, just as we do with all our thoughts, and come to a place where we are able to control what we can – our emotional responses, and our compulsions. Our beliefs and thoughts are largely outside of our control and do not reflect the real pieces of who we are. Only our choices - our actions - are fully within our control. In time, our chosen actions become who we are. ERP helps sufferers to reduce the affective responses to our thoughts and thus our compulsions resulting from that felt anxiety.

Due to my triggers being largely internal – my memories, stories I had been told, mistakes I had made – ERP was not effective for me. If I discovered a specific trigger that recurred in my environment, I could expose myself repeatedly until I was desensitized to it, effectively experiencing less anxiety as a result. Unfortunately, being largely unobservant by nature, most of my triggers were not environmental. It seemed that more action-oriented treatment, such as focusing on my actions alone, as well as working on my core beliefs and sense of self-trust was what carried me. I had to accept uncertainty but also a level of trust that I would make the right decisions in my life regarding my values. This took a long time, but I became stronger. These are largely premises of Acceptance and Commitment Therapy, which has also been shown to be effective for the treatment of OCD.

The best treatment for OCD has been shown to be a combination of therapy and medication. Though Selective-Serotonin Reuptake Inhibitors (SSRIs) is the designated medication for OCD, as it is for anxiety and depression, studies have shown that usually, OCD needs higher doses to effectively treat OCD symptoms, in comparison to anxiety or depressive disorders – another reason it is crucial to properly diagnose OCD. I consider myself lucky, because once I had the right diagnosis, medication, and dosage, my medication worked wonders in being able to resist my urges and control compulsions. It did not reduce my obsessions, but it did reduce my anxiety that resulted from the obsessions, and it made it possible for me to recover. And I only needed possible.

The self-help book that was largely effective for me was *The OCD Workbook* by Bruce Hyman. It taught me what I needed to understand about OCD to recover and eventually heal. OCD is largely about resisting the power of your thoughts. Because resisting compulsions can be chemically and behaviorally similar to resisting drugs and alcohol, OCD Anonymous (OCDA) exists to provide similar support to those in need. These meetings are anonymous, as they are conducted via phone seven days a week. OCDA helps sufferers accept that they have no power over their thoughts and that in order to recover, we must have faith in something beyond ourselves.

There are treatments for OCD, but any successful treatment is going to largely include being your own therapist. Those of us who have recovered from this treacherous disorder are the best therapists out there for it. Nobody – no therapist, even – quite understands OCD like those who live with it.

12 Steps of OCD Anonymous

Step 1. We admitted we were powerless over our obsessions and compulsions - that our lives had become unmanageable.

Step 2. Came to believe that a power greater than ourselves could restore us to sanity.

Step 3. Made a decision to turn our will and our lives over to the care of God, as we understood him.

Step 4. Made a searching and a fearless moral inventory of ourselves.

Step 5. Admitted to God, to ourselves, and to another human being the exact nature of our wrongs.

Step 6. Were entirely ready to have God remove all these defects of character.

Step 7. Humbly asked god to remove our shortcomings.

Step 8. Made a list of all persons we had harmed and became willing to make amends to them all.

Step 9. Made direct amends to such people wherever possible, except when to do so would injure them or others.

Step 10. Continued to take personal inventory and when we were wrong promptly admitted it.

Step 11. Sought through prayer and meditation to improve our conscious contact with god as we understand god, praying only for knowledge of gods will for us and the power to carry that out.

Step 12. Having had a spiritual awakening as the result of these steps, we tried to carry this message to those who still suffer from obsessive compulsive disorder, and to practice these principles in all our affairs.

OCD is chronic. It is not to be cured, only managed. With a ton of dedication, effort, and education, it can be managed well – but that may look different for everyone.

Knowledge is everything – it saved my life, and I think it has the potential to save many. Education is crucial due to the prominence and consequences of misdiagnosis in OCD and the need for a deep understanding of self for those who suffer from this disorder. As mentioned, OCD is one of the more common mental illnesses, and the understanding of the true nature of this illness can minimize stereotypes and ignorance, thus also minimizing the isolation felt by those who live it.

Awaken

My psychiatrist, in the little time we spent together, guided me, and I lived by that guidance. During one session, he said, "there's what is going on in your head – and it may always be there – but you also have to question 'is doing that going to make me the person I want to be?' You have a choice."

Coming out of it, as the medication took effect and my realization of what my thoughts were grew, it was how others have described it. It was like waking up, but it wasn't fast. First, I recognized colors being brighter than I remembered. Then, beauty in a way I had never seen before. And finally, I felt. It was like waking up from an all-night dream where I was paralyzed. You know you're paralyzed, and you don't believe you'll ever, ever wake up. You can't see the colors of the sky above you. You can't hear the person talking about their day next to you. You can't think about the material covered in the class you are sitting in.

When you go for so long in conflict with reality, dissociated, you accept that you don't know which feelings and thoughts are real. And which ones are tricks of that head demon, that overactive brain we OCDers have. In awakening, I began to guess which parts were real and which parts were not.

Some things weren't real:

o   Amanda and my family didn't want rid of me; they were merely scared for me and **doubt**ed their ability to help me.

o   My thoughts were not prophetic messages trying to push me into doing things I didn't want to do. They weren't helping me to avoid large tragedies. They were, and still are, random products of a chemical imbalance.

o   I was never at risk of killing myself. I was so scared at one point, in fear that I would, that I got a tattoo on my leg which symbolizes the promise to myself to never do so. That is how scared I was that *that* obsession was true, and how much **doubt** I had in my ability to overcome it.

o   I wasn't a terrible person, or a weak person. I was a sick one. My loved ones really did love (not hate) me.

And some things were real:

o   Friendships were over, and others would never be the same.

o   More than anything, I would never be the same. Years of my life were stolen.

o   I had found true love, and I had to work to feel and accept that I deserved it. If I didn't, I would destroy it, and almost did.

Looking back to understand what had happened in the last decade of my life, things looked differently. They looked clear, and that was a very difficult thing to bare. I had made all my bigger, important decisions based on the fear and **doubt** that OCD had instilled in me, and I could not get those back. My decisions of a decade suddenly had a clear pattern that I had to acknowledge and understand to prevent similar patterns in my future. I had to build a trust in my own decision-making that, for as long as I can remember, I hadn't had.

I write about me, because I think that the 'me' was a large part of the reason OCD was able to take refuge inside my mind, twisting everything inside of it over time. The parts of me I was born with, the parts of me I developed and nurtured, things I can't change and things I wish I could.

I seek depth. My greatest interest, amongst so many others, is crime. Sometimes, I can't even sleep unless I am watching *Criminal Minds* or some other drama about serial killers. I love getting deep into the head of other people, and after learning about human psychology, criminal justice, forensics, and profiling for much of my life, I can read people quite naturally. I was reading about murder when I was young, I would sneak shows in which adults did unpredictable things, and the more intense a movie was, the better.

But I do need meaning. I hate when there is no *purpose* to the violence in a show or movie. Just sex and violence lacking meaning. I want a story, I want to know about the people involved, and I want to understand the process of getting to the conclusion. I can take brutality if it demonstrates an amazing survivor story, integrity, honor, something. Give me the backgrounds of the people in the show as well as the victims and perpetrators. And this really goes for any part of my life – I want to dig deep. I tend to analyze everything, and people often think that is because of my job. Sure, it makes me good at my job, but it is because of me. It is who I am. My light, my strength has always become most evident within the darkness.

I am intense. A friend gave me the task once to be light, casual, not so serious. She asked me to write a children's book. I put my all into it, a tale of fantasy with the classic lesson thrown into the tale.

When my friend read it, she said that I should never write anything for a child. That they would only have nightmares. I heeded the advice.

I am a learner, and I have always been more drawn to the dark side of things; these things specifically contributed to my worsening symptoms. My brain chemistry interacted with what was happening in my life and how I was *responding to* both, and just like I believe it does in every situation, it created a monster. To have OCD, we must perceive and feel our thoughts more fully. To have psychosis, we must consider our thoughts so deeply that they become delusions. Something about me believed my head – maybe because I had always been able to trust it to such a degree, in other ways. Maybe because I analyze so very deeply – I couldn't have things just going on in my head and not pay attention to them.

I am an overachiever. I have a need to know, do, and experience as much as I can, especially in the areas I feel passion for - where I feel myself come alive. Travel, academia, writing, and literature. More than anything, I've wanted to know and define myself. My grandmother once told me that I was the most self-aware person she has ever known, and I score highest in intrapersonal intelligence – knowledge of self – on multiple intelligences tests. And thus, when my OCD began as a whisper, I needed to dig through every thought and urge and feeling I had, analyzing, exploring, and resolving what they were trying to tell me. I needed to solve the puzzle even when my thoughts became louder. I wanted to solve it so that my mind would stop – stop the thoughts of torment and worst-case-scenarios and the resulting feelings of doom. I wanted it to stop so badly that I literally drove myself to psychosis.

Please don't get me wrong. There is no choice inside of a mental illness. To say "choice" implies one is consciously deciding, and nobody decides this. I didn't choose to have the genetic makeup to produce OCD. I didn't choose to be as serious as I am or to grow up in a house that nurtured anxiety. I didn't choose the way my mind works, and I didn't choose who I love. But I did choose to realize that because I am who I am, it left me vulnerable to the demon that had always been there, waiting for its chance. By admitting my vulnerability, I gave myself the strength of awareness. Only in the awareness of how I fed it did I begin to understand how to starve it and prevent accidentally feeding it again.

Weeks after getting my diagnosis and being treated, I acknowledged a hard truth. There is something inside of me, something more dangerous than my deep or analytical characteristics.

Something that would appear each time I deeply, passionately wanted something from life and was about to get it. Then, it would show its ugly face. It was an impulse. It took me years of medications, therapists, and just about every penny I could spare to realize the real issue. Despite surviving, despite hospitalization, despite finally finding a medication that worked to detach emotionally from my painful and horrifying thoughts, despite understanding that I have an obsessive mind, I still felt it. The impulse that would not leave as long as I possessed anything that I deeply desired. The impulse to destroy.

There is a proposed diagnosis called self-defeating personality disorder. Over the last few decades, it has been stated several times that self-defeating personality disorder warrants diagnostic consideration. The self-defeating personality may "avoid or undermine pleasurable experiences, be drawn to situations or relationships in which they will suffer and prevent others from helping them." In the midst of my OCD, I could have qualified for this due to the simple fact that I seemed to be so incredibly self-sabotaging. But as any mental health therapist will probably tell you, having *symptoms* of a disorder doesn't mean you "have" it. I have OCD and anxiety, but I also have had one symptom of this illness, three from that one, and many from some other ones. And you do, too.

We all do. But a symptom doesn't make a mental illness. What does, in every single mental illness you will find, is one qualification: it impairs your life in your ability to function.

OCD is not self-defeating personality disorder, but it is defeating. It leaves you guilty, ashamed, in **doubt**, and it takes the good parts of both you and your life. It pops up at the very best times. My worst times, outside of when I went to the hospital was after I found Amanda, after we got engaged, after starting my career as a professor, and right before we got married. My worst times were our best times.

This is not a characteristic you can read in a book or learn from a therapist who does not themselves have OCD. Only we insiders know this - you have to know its game and learn to be one step ahead. It is self-sabotaging, and this was such a distinct function of mine. For about ten years, I didn't overachieve on purpose, because when I tried to, it emerged.

Self-defeating personality disorder has largely been debunked due to a lack of scientific support. But when something is proposed, it exists to a degree that it has been largely considered. Some people do possess these qualities, and I am willing to bet that individuals who have such sabotaging qualities do so as a response to a belief that they should not succeed, should not be happy, and essentially, should not thrive. Maybe it starts in their thinking, maybe their obsessions. And maybe not.

Some disorders may later be a different classification all together or found to not be a disorder at all. After all, being homosexual was once a diagnosable mental disorder because it was simply misunderstood. Borderline personality disorder, for example, is in definition a lifelong disorder as well – the most prevalent personality disorder with a prevalence rate around 6% – but at least 1 in 3 individuals who are diagnosed are treated successfully, no longer meeting qualifications for the disorder.

When I dropped out of my PhD program, I felt the anxiety leave. It must have been the right decision, I figured. But as I sit and write this, nine years later, I know that it wasn't. Not because of the action, but because of the reason behind it. Really, the lack of reason behind it. I was scared the anxiety and self-deprecating obsessions would not go away, and when I thought of leaving, they dissipated. So, I left.

This impulse was the first feeling I felt. The impulse to run from what I wanted most. Deep down, I now know, I didn't feel I deserved these things, which allowed me to follow this impulse to run from the best things – the things that would allow me fulfillment in life. And if I didn't feel the urge to run, it was to instead sabotage them in some other way. Once I felt this impulse to run from the very thing that I wanted most at 22, the anxiety hit. I was crippled by panic; every evening, I was crippled by its attacks. I couldn't sleep, eat, and I lost a ton of weight. I knew I "had to" leave because it wouldn't leave until I gave it up, until I made the decision. In my resisting this impulse, the anxiety would come, trapping me until I gave in.

But with OCD, we often overlook it as a problem. Why does it matter if you flick, tap, step, check, reassure? It doesn't seem to matter, or it is so deceptive for so long that by the time it is a problem – by the time it is causing bigger issues in your life, it is too late. You must dig yourself out, and likely, you will need the right help to do so.

When something was good, I knew the impulse would come even though I didn't understand what exactly it was that was "coming." It wouldn't always be paralyzing anxiety. One time, it was debilitating depression. But I was waiting for something bad to happen to the best things in my life. Over time, however, I realized that the "bad" was also that I was continually giving up my happiest moments and opportunities in response to the impulse, always by convincing myself that they were not "meant to be" for me. It wasn't just the urge; it was my response to it. And that was the part that I learned to control.

After I got divorced, I suddenly wanted things that I never let myself want before. I wanted a loving relationship where the person smiles each time they see me, where there is attraction and friendship, and for the very first time, I wanted children. I wrote down on a piece of paper the traits I wanted in a partner and the traits I would refuse to accept in one. My high school psychology teacher had told us that she had done this after her first divorce, and 12 years later, I did it after mine. I thought of the few relationships I had had, and the traits I would not accept again. I wanted someone who was funny, honest, kind, and didn't put work before family, and I did not want someone who drank, lied, ran from issues, or cheated.

I wanted these things, but I didn't plan to get them. I figured I would spend years alone, and this was good, because I knew that my life was best the way it was becoming – empty. The more purpose I felt, the more I had to lose. I accepted my life alone. I accepted, despite my desires, that I hadn't been a good partner and that I was best alone. Until I met Amanda.

There is a connection some people have where you not so much meet as rekindle an old connection, where it feels like you knew each other before. I knew she was the love of my life, and I immediately cherished her in the obvious way she also cherished me.

Amanda and I came from totally different relationship backgrounds. She had had very few relationships and a slew of dating through her 20s. She had come out at the age of 14, and I still was unsure of my label. I had few relationships, gotten married young, and was newly wounded from the obvious pains of divorce. I would've said I was really looking for casual, but what I had really asked the universe for, what I deeply desired, was sitting right in front of me. This girl is the girl I wanted all the things in my life with, and there was no **doubt**.

Unfortunately, people think that when you meet your person, that it is easy. I protest that it can be quite the opposite. Especially if you have been through a lot, the kind of love that burns fires and transcends struggle also brings to the surface all your own boundaries and insecurities. I read that soulmate love usually creates this runner-chaser dynamic because of fear, but it is also very difficult to really let go, because the love is encapsulating. Even if one leaves, the hearts are always tied, and neither will ever replace the other. And later when we separated, the only thing I knew and never once **doubt**ed was that I could not and would not be replaced, and nor could she. It was a knowing beyond anything I had ever experienced. I knew we would only get that love once.

Amanda triggered many recent wounds for me, wounds that I still was struggling to heal from. I suddenly felt things I never had before. Jealousy for some of her past and insecurity about my own. I pulled away a lot, because of the pain of my past, and because I do tend to pull away from good in my life, assuming it is going to go awry. After our first fight about nine months into dating, she took her turn at pulling away, and my anxiety reared its ugly head.

For a very long time, I was anxious and trying to "figure out" what the anxiety was trying to tell me. I was anxious because I was absolutely convinced that I would lose what I held most dear: Amanda. I knew something was coming. I replayed ways I could mess it up or things that could happen. I obsessed over one thing and then the other and my mind never stopped. And somehow, I knew it was related to what had happened with my PhD.

When I was diagnosed, I felt shamed and lost, but to get a label was a relief, and so was having a doctor who understood OCD. After a few weeks of medication, I felt a lift, and yet, without Amanda, I also felt heartbroken. We talked throughout our break, and after two months and with my continued improvement, we reunited. We were happy, and my anxiety and **doubt**ing were quickly becoming manageable. Little by little, I re-learned myself, and Amanda further helped me remember who I really am.

About a month into being back together, I began getting the impulse to run again and the obsessions got stronger. It didn't matter if it was a good day or bad day, though it did get worse when I was in pain, tired, or not feeling well. But for the very first time in my life, with far more manageable levels of anxiety, I saw this urge for what it was. I was on the outside looking in on it, rather than entrenched and tied down by it. A few times, my mother helped remind me and stabilize me – she would state that I was not rational, that I loved Amanda, and that Amanda had always been there for me. That my fear was causing this impulse to run away. Fear of worsening OCD, fear of a broken heart, and fear of what that broken heart could do to my mind. Us with OCD are always going to be at a greater risk of life's darkness eating us alive.

Eventually, it became easier. For many months, it was like resisting an itch. But I knew now - I knew what it was, and that knowledge truly gave me power. When my obsessions were strong, I knew it wasn't me; I had learned the difference between my thoughts and reality. My medication kept the intense anxiety at bay. I knew it wasn't about the topics in my head, but about running from the things I really wanted in life. Some days, I felt completely lost to it. But I made sure that most days, I was ready to face it. That I would never, ever give up what I wanted in response to it. That I would not give up my doctorate (the second time around), job opportunities that were going to present themselves, and especially not the person I wanted to spend every day of my life with.

Healing is not linear. It is up and down, down and up, up up up down down. It can be all over the place, without prediction or script. The problem is in the brain, and that brain is affected by everything. There have been more evenings than I could truly count that I cried myself to sleep, in which everything in my mind and body wanted to run or do something else impulsive that I knew wasn't the real me. Days in which I didn't even know what was happening, but I was just uncomfortable. Days when I wish I wasn't in my body. But over time, these days become less frequent and more predictable.

Over a four-month period, my doctor raised my medication dosage three times, finally ending at the maximum dosage. It was predictable, given that my symptoms had become severe, but it made me uncomfortable – where do I go if it stops working? How do I know it is truly the best drug for me? **Doubt.**

Every step of this process requires trust. Having a trusting and intelligent doctor who was passionate about OCD and its treatment, my questions were answered the best they could be. And when they couldn't be, as there are so many unanswered questions in medicine, he reassured me or rationalized with me. He reminded me who I was and what I wanted, and that this would always be up to me. If I knew its tricks, I could always play its game.

I do just that, and always will.

I had been working with children for almost two years – a population that I felt untriggered by and an easier way for me to still be contributing that didn't negatively impact my fragile mind. Mainly, I was a teacher, though I did also provide counseling sessions with children intermittently. After four months of treatment, I took a chance. As I was healing, I felt a desire I hadn't felt in years – to work as a social worker again. I took a job working part-time with homeless women and children as a clinical director at a local agency. It further challenged me in my healing process, and there were some bad days, but over time, it gave me a sense of purpose and fulfillment I had missed. Today, I still do some work with this organization as a therapist, passionate about the work that is being done to eliminate and heal the systemic issue of homelessness.

In a way that I couldn't after I began treatment, despite my best efforts, I became more able to tackle large goals. I successfully defended my doctoral research, worked two jobs, and six months later, I completed an entire day of professor interviews across the country.

Soon later, COVID-19 hit the United States, with Ohio being one of the first states to discover a case and one of the first to close. This day was March 13, and I was in Ohio. I was interviewing at a university for a professor position. This week, I was sick, anxious, and could barely focus on preparing. But, when I went, I did perfectly. Presenting my research as well as teaching a class on a subject I was passionate about – end-of-life – felt natural and exciting. I was essentially told that I had done fantastic, had gotten the job, and would hear back soon.

That evening, all public universities in the state of Ohio would close and remain closed for the year. I waited two months to hear from the program, and for two months, was emailed that all public university job offers in the state of Ohio were frozen and that there was no knowing if they would unfreeze.

In the past, this was the kind of unexpected event that would have floored me. Finally shooting for a job that I had dreamed of since I was a teenager, successfully attaining it in the state I wanted to live, and then *Bam*, the world stops.

Uncertainty is worse than a certain doom for those with OCD. While conducting research, I recently talked to a girl who, unknowingly, described to me the closest she had ever been to suicide in her countless considerations of it. In this time, she had a lot of fear of dying. It began with one thing – that she had drank enough alcohol to induce cirrhosis of the liver – and then she began obsessing about all the ways that she could die. Just as I had had such intense fear of losing my doctorate and then losing my partner, she had intense fear of dying. So, the mind devised every way it was possible for her to experience this.

In the *complete inability to handle the fear* – not the possibility of death itself – she had planned to take her own life. This is an example of how fear can be the absolute worst, most devastating feeling for people like me. We would rather face the worst possible circumstance than forever feel the feelings we are having from the endless thoughts we cannot control.

In the past, the uncertainty of my future job may have derailed my mental health. Every single person with OCD loves control – we obsessively **doubt** because we want to be able to control the future. But six months into treatment, I was a different person. I focused on what I could control and what I loved. I loved both of my jobs and decided that if I had to work them another year in lieu of becoming a professor, I would accept that. Acceptance and planning for the unplanned is a wonderful way to manage OCD.

In May, I was contacted by another university. After two interviews, I was hired with less than 8 weeks' notice to move from Florida to Colorado. Ten months after my diagnosis, we got in the car to do what I had always planned, and what we had planned for three years, together.

I can proudly say that in these past two years, I have been a source of strength inside my marriage. I have become the calm and level-headed person that I was meant to be and never could be before. A partner to be trusted, leaned on, and perhaps even someone worthy of love – though I still have my **doubt**s. They are a part of the human condition, after all, and have no value in the life that I live and the life that I am always planning. Just like the demon that waited to be fed, the best pieces of me were there all along, waiting to be unleashed, waiting to be me.

Most people would say the worst thing they've experienced is something external. Something that happened. Someone they lost. Something someone did to them, or to someone else.

It is an odd thing for that worst thing to be inside of you. You don't escape it, nor does it leave. It shares your mind, your feelings, and it shares your energy. The more energy it consumes, the more it consumes you. And the less you have left.

OCD has held me back, in some ways that are difficult to express. **Doubt** of myself caused me to leave one program that meant the world to me and six years later, put me on the brink of leaving the next one as well. I had gotten rid of everything, thrown everything to the hungry wolf, and it still wanted more. It wanted me. And in some sense, I had to let it have me, let it kill whatever was left of "me" to start over as a new me who survived, and then healed, and then thrived.

I realized that the impulse would come, no matter what I did. But what I associated it with – and choosing *not* to associate it with anything important – was up to me. And my actions were absolutely mine. Even if it felt some days like being tortured and still not succumbing, it was my choice. This time, this decade of my life, was going to be designed by Brittany, not OCD, and not the part of me that sabotaged *that* Brittany or her life.

My advice to others in recovery – from any mental illness that will likely never leave – is to find what works and to put your energy into the person you want to be, not the person it has made you. Viktor Frankl, the founder of logotherapy, proclaimed that the belief that we are only a product of biological, psychological, social forces is dangerous, because it gives us the illusion of not having choices. Only one thing determines who we are, and that is our actions. We do not make choices based on who we are, *we* are based on our choices.

Choose

One evening an old Cherokee told his grandson about a battle that goes on inside people. He said, "My son, the battle is between two 'wolves' inside us all. One is Evil. It is anger, envy, jealousy, sorrow, regret, greed, arrogance, self-pity, guilt, resentment, inferiority, lies, false pride, superiority, and ego. The other is Good. It is joy, peace, love, hope, serenity, humility, kindness, benevolence, empathy, generosity, truth, compassion, and faith." The grandson thought about it for a minute and then asked his grandfather: "Which wolf wins?" "The one you feed."

Cherokee Indian Tale

Sometimes I am angry. So angry.

For what OCD has taken from me, the choices I have allowed it to make for me, and that it will affect me moving forward.

I am angry that nobody believed me, and for what that cost me.

I am angry that some people get diagnosed with OCD in a day while I spent years trying to get help.

I am angry that I ended up in a hospital.

I am angry that if I have a child, the medication will have an unknown effect on the pregnancy.

I am angry that my life may always look and feel different with OCD.

I am angry that I have OCD.

———————

There are some choices I may never have.

I don't choose to feel anger.

I certainly did not choose to have a mental health disorder, or to have my obsessions derail 29 years of the choices I made.

I did not choose to have practitioners misdiagnose and under-diagnose me for years.

I do not choose to require medication to feel like myself, to function fully, to come back to reality.

I did not choose to love a woman.

But I do choose how I live these choices.

I did choose to advocate endlessly for my own treatment.

I did choose to find and trust my doctor when I did.

I choose to take the medication I know I need. The medication that allows me to live my life.

I did choose to honor and spend my life with that woman.

Aside from faith, only choice brought me from the floor of a hospital, crumbling under the psychosis of my mind, to being a professor in one year's time. Choice alone brought me to the life I had wanted, and it is the only thing that brings any of us what we truly desire.

My thoughts did not completely or forever go away, and to this day, I have no choice when or what they are. But I always have the choice not to feed them.

———————

I choose to advocate.

As time went on, I felt a pressing obligation to confront the egregious treatment of my last therapist. With time, I became more of myself and that meant bolder, wiser, and I gained a heck of a lot of clarity. I could see what I had said and done, and how erratic I was in my final days, but I could also see the actions of others more clearly.

Confronting a therapist is like a mix of confronting your teacher, your parent, and your priest. They are supposed to guide, encourage, and participate in healing you. They are supposed to have unconditional positive regard for you, no matter what. But more so than anything, they are never, ever to do you harm. Which is why it is so important that therapists and practitioners alike know what they are doing and do not ever breach areas they are not competent to treat.

In my last session with this therapist, I made it a point to bring with me the feelings I had about the things she had said when I was ill. The things that I had only said and done – things I had *only* blamed myself for until now – with her encouragement and support. That OCD had become me because of these choices of hers as well. I told her that I was saying these things because I would want to know, as a therapist, if I had harmed a client and could do better for future clients. I told her that I felt that she made my OCD worse, that she did not *ever* accept, validate, or treat my diagnosis – despite having asked directly if she could treat it – and that it had done me harm. And most of all, that I never felt I could tell her the truth, because of her defensiveness and denial.

She denied having said the things that I told her had hurt me. She claimed she did not remember saying these things. I told her she had directly invalidated me once by saying "why do they upset you, they are just thoughts" when really, that statement was the very definition of OCD. She disagreed and again, denied any responsibility.

After our last session, I changed my phone number and email address. Though I had healed so much, I still felt susceptible to people like my therapist. I changed my information because I had actual fear of what further conversations and contact from her – in memory of the things she had said and things she encouraged of me – would do to my psyche.

People with OCD are so very susceptible to mere words. We live in fear of relapse. We live in a fear of what the wrong thing said could do to our stability if our minds grab hold. Sure, we can control our reactions, but we largely cannot control our thoughts, and resulting feelings.

With the encouragement of a later therapist, I reported my therapist to the state licensing board. I reported her with the kind of guilt a child of a narcissistic parent feels, with the thought of what she would say in my mind… 'but I tried to help you, why would you do this to me?' But I did it for every single person with a developing mental illness who may end up as her client and possibly at the end of what they can tolerate of suffering. I reported in hopes she would never work with those who have a serious mental health disorder again and if she did, she would now understand how much dangerous power she has to not just help, but to hurt.

Unfortunately, nothing ever came from my report, as far as I know. The state told me that to investigate my report, they would have to divulge my contact information to my old therapist. This forced me to then report anonymously, knowing it would not go further. I hope every day that my letter had the effect it needed.

———————————

I choose my label. Not the diagnosis, but I do choose the label.

I respect the avoidance of using labels. Sometimes, they only cause harm to the individual. But this is case by case. Would you treat a physical ailment without knowing its name? Probably not, and more so, not effectively. If you don't know the problem, you are only guessing at the solution. I have talked with a lot of clients, students, researchers who have had a consensual opinion about practitioners who do not want to diagnose: *they were not helpful.* They were nice, and they certainly did not harm (since they clearly avoid pushing hard enough to really risk that), but they did not help. There is power in labels. Inside a therapy room, I say, let's label the hell out of ourselves. Because then we can learn, and understand, and fix or stabilize. We can sometimes get rid of the label completely. Or we can know for sure that the label is not helpful.

But you cannot know without one.

In the past, I have run from life-sentencing labels, but there is power in them. In this power, I know that my obsessions have no meaning. I know that I control how much energy, attention, and response I give to them. I know the treatment, and I know what helps. I know how to help others, because I know how to help myself.

I also know that it is chronic. I know that sometimes, it makes relationships harder, and when things are good, I need to be ready.

I choose to let go.

After all, letting go is the key. Acceptance is the key. *Refusing*, every time, to appraise the thoughts or fear as important is a practice needed to overcome – to reform the mind and how I respond to it. Thoughts are not chosen, and when someone has a thought disorder like OCD, they most definitely don't have meaning. Actually, they tend to have the opposite meaning of who the person really is. I have always been a loyal and honest person and yet, events in my life severely damaged my sense of self trust. And then, I **doubt**ed myself, everything good, everything loyal. I thought maybe my thoughts meant I couldn't be honest or loyal or a good partner – all the things I was and always wanted to be.

The key for me was accepting and loving me. Loving that my differences meant I would always be unfulfilled in shallow relationships, that break ups would be catastrophically painful, and every time I felt shoved aside, it would feel like a bullet. Once, a friend "broke up" with me, and I cried every day for six months. I "moved on" with life, but emotionally, I was always a wreck when these things would happen – especially prior to my treatment. I would look at others throughout my life and be so envious that they could just let go of the bad in life.

I woke up one morning to realize how far my life had come in a matter of months. I was with a person I loved dearly – and who loved me the way I deserved – and I was months away from graduating with my doctorate. Both were second chances for me at the two things I wanted most. I had chosen the easy route in both letting go of my PhD and marrying young, both I knew to be the safe options. And now, I was sitting with two more things I had nearly let go of in fear – my person and my degree. And this time, I saw that I had a choice. That I would always have a choice. To be happy or to be safe. To be fulfilled or to be comfortable.

Every single day, multiple times, OCD makes me choose. Between comfort, and the life I want and person I want to be. My obsessions surround the things that matter most in my life, and it has taken me a long time to realize that they are empty thoughts – that they hold no intuition or higher meaning or indication of a road to take. Compulsing, for me, would mean sabotaging my life, as I have before. Each day when OCD is active, I choose who to be. Some days, it's almost easy, sometimes it's exhausting, and sometimes I'm a wreck. But I will always win.

I choose to accept judgment and live regardless of it. Others will never really know my demons.

It is impossible to know what goes on inside another's mind. It can be an entire world. I will never truly know the color or shape of my partner's world and what demons lie in wait there. But now, I do know there are demons. In everyone's worlds.

As I was recovering, I felt judged by certain people. I'd like to say I was judged by people who saw the worst of it, or people who didn't understand mental illness, or people who somehow had a place to judge. But it's not true. Unfortunately, when you've been deteriorating for so long, you are always to blame in the minds of others. They don't know which parts were *you,* but they give you ownership for all of them.

Fundamental attribution error is the tendency for outsiders of a situation to overestimate the role of the actor's behaviors and underestimate situational causes. Therefore, it is natural for us to look at situations, such as a person's mental illness, and incorrectly put more blame on the person than on the situation. Of course, in the case of ourselves, it is the opposite. We more so blame the situation and not ourselves. Usually, neither is completely accurate.

After being diagnosed, after I was OK, I realized that because I was so open – because I sought so much reassurance and had talked to so many people, it gave those who did not understand my struggle, perhaps those who did not really care to try to understand, a lot of opportunity to judge. When I was healing, I became aware of the judgments I had not seen before. Key people in my life fell away, and relationships with some others were forever changed.

It would be a lie to say I understand people who turn away when someone close to them is in pain, because I cannot. But I can accept that people have no clue how to handle things. Some people don't know what to say or do. This, I know. But the judgment, I don't get. Realizing that someone was suffering due to an illness, not acting or being weak or hurting others, and then judging – this, I struggle to grasp. But I do choose to accept it.

I decided that I will not entertain judgment from others who do not know me, were not there for me, and those who do not confront me with the goal to understand. I grew up in a family where we say what we think and feel, and I am a product of that authentic style. My family expresses their hurt with the goal to work things out. With the goal to control, maybe. To understand.

But never to judge. It is far more healthy than passive aggression, gossip, and disingenuous manners. This style has no purpose but to judge – it seeks superiority and contempt. Because that is not who I am, I choose not to play the game. I am always willing to discuss my past, my truths, my illness - even when I should not have to - to anyone who cares enough to want to repair their perceptions of me or try to understand me, and if they are not brave enough to have that conversation with me, that is a reflection on them. Not me.

When you have a mental illness, when you are sensitive, when you have trauma and feel a lot of pain, it is important to make the active choice of who you have in your life. Family may be there either way, but the relationship and time spent is a choice. Nobody is perfect, and all will make mistakes, and for those who love you, it will be an anomaly. They won't want to hurt you, but they do hurt too, and sometimes hurt is shared.

Someone once said to me that they didn't understand why I suffered so – "after all, you weren't raped or anything." That's when I realized that nobody really would understand the pain of the mind playing tricks on you, torturing you with its thoughts, its obsessions. As my psychiatrist says, OCD is closer to schizophrenia than anything else, in the way that it presents. It's a thought disorder, and it will never be understood. With some strength, I later responded to that person that I would *rather* have

153

been raped, I would rather almost anything. Almost anything with an ending. So then, there would be an end, there would be a defined course of treatment, and there would be remission and healing. That one day, it would be a memory, no longer in my body or in my mind. Instead, I have no remission, only acceptance. I recover, I pick myself up from the ground, but my mind still works differently, and the world is still one big trigger. We all have scars and memories. But I must live with the probability of relapse, the reality of medication, and with my monster being inside the prison of my own mind.

———————

I choose to be grateful. Some days, I fail. Some days, I feel anything but grateful. But I choose to be as grateful as possible by focusing on what I *do* have, *because* I have experienced all that I have.

Despite the pain and the fact that I know I must live with the **doubt** and anxiety that provokes my mind. Some days, it is even natural - I *feel* grateful.

My experience has changed me. I have more compassion, empathy, kindness, and humor than ever before. In knowing there is some part of my mind that is dark and out to sabotage my best self, the other part of me – the stronger part, forevermore – has grown softer, kinder. I love that part of me – the real me – more than I ever could love what was there before. It has made me so irrevocably aware of true pain. The best bridge to compassion for others is suffering in oneself.

My mild OCD symptoms through my life made me tough and insensitive. Neurotic, prone to irritation and anger. On the other hand, when my symptoms became worse, I didn't have the energy to be these things. I became soft, and I went from being a person who had to actively make the effort to *be a little gentler, a little more sensitive, realize how my words could hurt* to being the girl who had to *try* to be tough. It was no longer natural to be a fighter; after all, I had to fight every single day to survive, to function. In my recovery, I found balance for the first time in my life. I was understanding, yet tough. I was smart and perceptive, yet I chose my words and actions carefully. I became the best version of myself, also accepting myself as so far from perfect.

I am one of the lucky ones. After a very long time, my medication worked to quiet my thought demons. It took months on medication and finding the right dose, but I realized then that I was finally *mostly* in control of the thoughts. Just as I was considering an experimental hallucinogenic or doing just about anything to add to the moderate improvement I had made, Bam. Six months exactly, and the thoughts were slipping away.

My therapist said something around this time that made perfect sense for me – she said that when someone develops OCD, it is because they have had such intense emotional pain which cannot be handled or processed by their body that their mind fractures instead. The mind takes the pain on itself, and it fractures.

I chose, and choose, to fight.

I chose to use every resource I could possibly find, every ounce of strength inside of me to support the only ending I would allow. I went to therapy, I got neurofeedback and hypnosis, I planned my future, I travelled, I took my medication, and I learned. I found out everything I could about OCD, and I used it. I found that therapy itself was the least helpful of everything I tried. Of course, my therapist was not adept at treating OCD, and the OCD group therapy sessions I attended were more than unhelpful – they were triggering. Today, I can listen to the experiences of other people with this illness – though always carefully, timidly - but at that time, I could not. Sitting in a group – which already was uncomfortable to me – while other people fed us ideas of how different forms of OCD could look and how much they had suffered - was too emotionally difficult for me.

With all the efforts, one day, I realized that I felt normal again. That I had hours at a time in which I didn't have a bad thought or even fear a bad thought. That when I did have one, I could let it pass without feeling I needed to analyze it. With medication, and with the slow learning process of getting used to the way my mind worked – and not taking it seriously – I moved on. I lived.

Recovering from my hell was the hardest and the slowest process of my life. It's not that I didn't think I could survive – sometimes, I just wished I wouldn't so that I didn't have to live with this.

Some experiences change a person. So profoundly, in fact, that it's like walking into a place you no longer recognize. Almost every relationship was somehow different. It's like you wake up and smile and everyone is glad you are back - some disappeared while you were gone, and others pretend you never left - but you know you aren't the same person. You know that on one of those days, probably one of those really, really bad days, a part of you that makes you *you* left, and she is not coming back. You are different in a way you could never put into words. Maybe it's how soldiers feel when they've been to war – in a different world for so very long – and nothing seems safe when they get back. But it is hard to believe it, and even harder to adjust. Things look different and **everything** feels different.

I felt completely detached from my life after recovering. I felt different – in a good way – but everything around me was a reminder. Within a month of diagnosis, I changed jobs. Within two months, I had my partner back. Within four, I was a therapist again. I changed my hair, I got rid most of my things. I applied to jobs out-of-state, and I waited to move, counting down each day. I liked living again, perhaps more than ever, but I had to begin again. Within 11 months, thanks to my doctors, my own perseverance, and my family, I was moving to Colorado to accept a job offer as a professor.

I choose faith.

Even when someone is healed, there still lies a susceptibility. My OCD always came at the best moments of my life, and knowing this, when I plan for the best moments, I stand guard like a watchman. I plan a wedding, and I hold my breath. I become a professor and I graduate with my doctorate, and I hold my breath. I move away and plan to have a child, and more than anything before, I wait. It's like having a dangerous ex who you know is out there, and will probably come back for you one day, and you just don't know when. You know the old games, but who knows. Maybe there will be a new one. Or maybe they won't come back?

Before OCD took my life, I used to feel that anything that came my way, I could handle. That I couldn't break. I was proud of my strength and convinced of it. Today, I don't believe that. We are all breakable. I don't mean that we can't survive, just that something in us dies. There is something for all of us that'll do it. Many things, actually. So, for me, I ask the universe, to just not give me the same thing again. I've survived once, it has changed me forever, is with me forever, and I promise to use it to make me better – kinder, stronger, a better mother and partner and friend. I will focus on what it has given me and not dwell on what it has destroyed.

I choose me.

Perhaps nobody is truly sure of themselves. That those of us with big hearts, who love easily and love many, feel confusion. And the more you try to figure out how to define yourself, the more confused you can get. Because the truth is that *you are undefinable.* You are not a definition, a set of words. There is no explanation of *you.* You are profound, vast, and abstract as hell. You cannot be found by looking at another, being with another, in the presence of another, though sometimes you can find what you are *not* with the help of another.

I figured out that I am not my mind. I am not my confusion or my past or my sexuality. I am so much more than any of it. I am a partner. I am clumsy. I am foolishly gullible at times. I am hard on myself. I am intelligent. I am an academic, a writer. I have a big heart. I am my family and the love I have in my heart for them. I am my actions today, not yesterday. I am me.

So, what did I learn? That I cannot find myself in another, or inside my own mind. I can, however, lose myself in both. The person who must love me the most is the person I am stuck with. Me. I have learned a lot, but there will always remain more. More insecurities, more triggers, more possibilities for **doubt.** The things I need to do, only I can do. The things I need to learn, only I can learn.

Let go.

Trust.

Love.

Allow myself to be happy.

I deserve to be happy.

Heal

Real love is absolutely everything. Most people have that kind of love for their children. Fewer for their spouses. My wife is my world, and long ago, I knew I would do absolutely anything for her. In ways she probably doesn't even know. And despite this love that deepens the cavern of our hearts, mental illness can shatter absolutely everything else. Everything that makes that love work.

Knowing this, I got her out. I did things knowing it would end with her leaving. I allowed myself to finally fall, but not until she left, just to be sure. I drove to the hospital, I didn't allow her to visit, and the next day, I drove to the home I knew she would leave. Any doubts about what she would do, how she would survive were gone. Now, apart from me, I knew she would be OK. She would be OK, because I had hurt her to save her from the demon that was inside of my head. The one who already had me. The one who wanted her too.

Things in my head, in my environment meant more than they actually meant. In reality, they meant nothing. But *I knew* they meant everything. All of it was a plan, a plan to take her by taking me. A grand scheme. To go into the deep and surely never come out. Only by making her leave could I let it have me, but me alone.

This is psychosis.

To perish and thus, survive.

And maybe, just *maybe,* heal.

A Letter to my Loved Ones

Winter 2019

To all who have seen me through a very difficult time, and all who may not have known.

I am writing this because despite wanting to isolate myself as I have been doing, I feel the need to explain something nobody here is going to understand. To apologize for related behaviors. Something I have always valued about myself is my authenticity, so though it makes me uncomfortable – and likely you as well - I feel the need to say it.

One April, I began experiencing bad anxiety. It had been growing worse since I got divorced, and after a small trigger, it went into full swing. I forced myself to be functional, mostly for my partner's sake and so I could work to pay my mortgage, but I barely was some days. It went up and down for a long time, but last summer, it went into full swing. It robbed me of so much, and worst of all, my self-love and my identity.

I would sometimes wake up and didn't recognize the person in the mirror. I quit being a social worker, a job that had given me purpose. I came close to giving up on school, which would likely have been my last chance of doing what I wanted to do and become a professor. After a long time helping me deal with it, I was also choosing to separate from my partner who made me happy in every moment she could. I was disappearing, and I didn't know why. In the final days, I was so stuck in my head that I didn't know which world was real.

One horrific morning, just shy of my 30th birthday, I left work and drove myself to the hospital. I didn't tell my family or partner because I didn't want to be stopped, and I didn't want any more burden to be put on them. After extensively leaning on others, I knew that whatever answer I was going to get, I would do it alone. After 4 therapists and 3 psychiatrists had shed every layer they could up until that point, I was still only getting worse. And I was tired of being told that I was OK when I knew that I wasn't. I was so full of **doubt** for every aspect of my life and myself that I finally just needed to do something and go through with it.

That week, I was finally diagnosed with obsessive-compulsive disorder. I felt relief to have a good doctor, an answer, and a path to start on. My doctor had looked at me and told me that this is a disorder that would make me feel isolated and one that almost nobody would understand the torture of. That OCD is a thought disorder that makes everything feel unreal, unsure, even right down to who you are. With this, I knew he was the right doctor. He knew not only the symptoms to look for, but the true nature of this disorder. You see, I don't clean or ritualize, I obsess and perform mental rituals.

We all have bad thoughts. Really bad thoughts. This I know. But for someone with this isolating form of OCD - mostly inside our heads - the thoughts *stick*. This part of the brain is extremely overactive. Common manifestations of Pure O are its sufferers worrying they are pedophiles, endlessly questioning if they are gay or straight, obsessing over taboo sexual acts, being convinced they are going to harm others in various ways - sticking their cats in microwaves, stabbing their child. But instead of this horrible thought passing, it sticks. It repeats and repeats and repeats. Thousands of times a day. The list of OCD obsessions goes on and on, and I don't need to say which ones I have experienced, but this I can tell you: OCD has a way of sticking to a thought that is oppositional to your true nature. If someone adores children, they are more likely to have pedophilia OCD, for example. Its job is to rob you of the things that most define you.

OCD used to be called the **doubt**ing disease. Its sufferers are riddled with **doubt** and uncertainty on Every Level. By the time I was diagnosed, I was convinced these thoughts were real. I thought they were commands from some higher power, things I needed to do. Reflections of who I was, in contrast to the real me, which had very much disappeared. Things that changed how I saw myself.

With my diagnosis, I finally had the power to say, 'It's not me, it's OCD.' On medication, the thoughts become manageable

165

background noise. But most people in recovery take six months to one year to slowly realize that their thoughts have no true meaning, and to feel they can enjoy life again. If they are lucky. It has been five months, though felt like five years, and I am getting there. But even now, I have thoughts that stick. To rewire years of paralyzing anxiety and mental compulsions is taking me a lot of time, as is loving myself again despite the shame I have for this part of me and the terrible version of me it created. I am working on literally rewiring my brain while the medication changes its chemistry.

I am writing this because I have tried to connect to others regarding what I deal with, and I was tired of feeling isolation when they over-identify with this illness. It doesn't even make me angry - it makes me so incredibly sad that what I cope with is *so* misunderstood that the person I am talking to believes they suddenly have it.

This is the norm response. Unless talking to a clinician, everyone has it. They confuse all full-blown diagnoses with a symptom. You arrange things or must have a clean kitchen, and you're OCD, right?

Wrong. Nobody with OCD – especially in its severest form - wants other people to relate. We wouldn't wish it on you. I know that OCD is more common than bipolar disorder or schizophrenia, making it crucial that we all understand what it looks like…but not everyone has it. *And this is a good thing.* OCD is not collecting things…unless that collection means you can't reach your bed. OCD is cleaning until your hands grow raw, and you keep going. Because if you don't, something bad will happen. Your family will get sick. Or something that makes no sense to anybody but you – your spouse will be in a car crash – *may* happen. Or, if the OCD grows severe, *will* happen.

These misunderstandings isolate those of us who suffer from mental illness. You do not understand the desire for someone's grief because you lost your parents. You do not understand OCD because you are Type A. You do not understand having bipolar because you change your mind a lot. Know that you know nothing – even if you have *the exact same illness* – because every person has different symptoms, different traumas, different demons that attack. Don't relate, don't tell. Listen.

The other reason for my isolation is because I have shame. I have shame particularly around the people that I dragged through my anxiety and panic attacks for so very long. I have shame that I needed help from my family, even for a short time, to be able to financially recover. I'm filing my taxes this week, and last year alone, I spent almost half my net income – very little, as I am a teacher right now - on medical bills alone. I have shame that I had to check myself into a hospital to get help - and to get my family to believe that I absolutely needed it. I am ashamed that I was sinking. I have shame that my mind works differently. I have shame that I cry a lot, trying to accept who I am, and that OCD has clung to the most important parts of my life and nearly destroyed them. Trying to have trust that it won't happen again, that I am stronger than it, is the battle of my life, and for now, it is every day.

The grief I have for the time lost, the friends lost, the feeling of being connected to myself and my life, is profound. Everything around me is a reminder of my worst days, and I am still having a difficult time connecting and feeling safe around others. Anything can be a trigger to my thoughts. I have an even harder time helping others like I used to. Children are the only ones I don't feel this with. I know that people don't trust me like they used to. See me like they used to. Some of my closest relationships are forever gone or forever changed. I am still recovering, and I still can't be at my best. I went from being somewhat of an extrovert to a loner in the years of undiagnosed Hell. OCD leads to avoidance. Intense, dire, panic-stricken avoidance that sometimes is livable, sometimes not, but always unfunctional.

I graduate with my doctorate, a journey that has taken me over ten years, in May. It's funny how little joy someone can get from big things in life when they feel so much pain. I plan to move and start over, away from all the reminders that don't let me move on. I want to start over in a place where everyone and everything doesn't remind me of the person I had become and the person I lost and wish I could be again, as well as the real-life traumas that triggered me into the fractured self I am still rebuilding.

I hope that this allows understanding. Not just for me, but for all people, because there are far too many people out there who suffer in silence. Misunderstood by others and filled with shame, and thus, alone. Let's fight the silence by allowing space for those who are suffering.

It took about six months before I felt I could again work with other people's pain. To feel that I had the capacity again to provide space to others in their moments of distress. And even then, it took even longer before I felt comfortable in doing so.

At first, I had anxiety and sadness. Working with the pain of adults was something I hadn't done for years. Children have pain, of course, but the resilience that children have is beyond that of adults. It was no longer play or fun that encouraged healing, as it was with children – it was talking. Talking about, processing, thinking about, and really empathizing with another's pain was effort on a level that I had not felt able to provide in years.

But with time, less anxiety, and more understanding of how my mind works, I learned to again practice a skill that had been there prior to my breakdown – compartmentalization. And the other skills came more naturally as my pain decreased.

As a therapist, we don't just work with the emotions of others. We use ourselves throughout practice to evoke things in our clients. To build a relationship that is the foundation of all effective therapy. To relate, to empathize. The techniques, the theories that one holds do not produce most of the healing that happens. The people in the room do. *We,* along with the clients, are the main tool for change.

Not only had I been unable to use myself, but I had also been unable to process, apply techniques, and deeply ponder the thoughts, emotions, and experiences of other people. I could barely have friends because I couldn't focus long on others. An effective therapist is one who has dealt with their own problems – because in *any* relationship, even that with a client, they will appear. They appear as lack of focus, as biases, in lacking emotion, or as emotional overload. As feeling stuck, which can come out as frustration, overprotectiveness, rejection. And above all, being fully present with a client is necessary to them feeling heard, understood, and validated, and thus, working toward healing.

Grief. That's what I've been working on for a while. It sure does look like depression. It is loss, it is pain, it is low, after all. But to be honest, there are important distinctions.

Grief signifies an ending. Depression may come from beginning, ending, or nothing at all. It just is. It may end tomorrow; it may never end.

Grief doesn't exclude the possibility of hope. It will never get worse than it has been, and yet, depression is open-ended. There is no knowing how much worse it can or will get until you're there, and then again, it's open-ended.

Grief, in short, is an emotional response to a loss – any loss. Of course, it is often associated with the loss of a person, however, there are other vital parts of life that can be lost and thus stimulate the grieving process.

The ability to grieve signifies the ability to be aware, to process, and to understand. It signifies life and survival while depression does not. And while it's literally taken years to process and accept the things I lost, I am grateful for the grief. I suffered for a long time in a state that would not have been able to grieve. I am grateful for feelings outside of anxiety, which used to rule every cell of my body, every second of my days. To feel sadness, to feel loss, to feel pain is a blessing.

This grief is a latter process to the anger I felt previously. But sometimes, I feel them both, intertwined inside my days, one closer to my heart, and then the other.

But normally, it's quiet. The kind of quiet and calm contemplation that the preceding anger didn't allow for.

Grieving is a normal life process, and it is also a normal recovery step, as detailed in *The OCD Workbook*:

It isn't unusual for those who make significant progress with their OCD in a relatively short time to go through a phase of feeling depressed. It's almost a state of bereavement: mourning for the years that were lost to OCD and the devastating toll it has taken. There may be a period of deep sadness and regret about what your life might have looked like had you recovered sooner. Forgive yourself and others for mistakes of the past. No life is ever perfect. Remember that without all those blind alleys, you would never have gotten to the point you are at today. They were an evitable part of your recovery. Use the painful past to further safeguard and solidify the recovery you've achieved now.

Aloneness is part of healthy grieving. Loneliness, however, is a different thing entirely and so very real when your mind has a whole world of its own. Even as you're rebuilding, the loneliness lives on. When you are forever different, sensitive, avoidant, and a purposeful loner, it doesn't leave. After I was diagnosed and began treatment, I was simply trying to feel my limbs again. I felt like I had been absent for a long, long time, and though there were days and moments in which I was there, I began to recognize the real world as the realest one. The only real one, in fact. With the whispers of the old beliefs still in my head and acknowledgement that the real parts of me that gave birth to them would always exist, I began to rethink, refeel, rebuild. And the hardest part was the refeeling. For a while, I couldn't figure out how I could cry so much and yet still feel flatter than ever before. I couldn't piece together how one could feel so numb and yet so full of every feeling. And I'm still not sure how much of it was due to, a response to, or completely unrelated to OCD. But it was grief.

What I was grieving, I can't be sure. My life. My love for my life. The feeling I had for it, or the feeling I thought I had for it. Feeling like my friends and family truly saw me. My partner. Everything looked differently on the other side. Everyone, even more.

In the coming months, I felt relief and growing strength. It would take six months for the anxiety and thoughts to ease, and then I would cope with this 'something else' of grief. The grief of the time lost, the smiles and experiences lost. I had been to Paris during the breakdown, I had gotten engaged during the breakdown, I had had an entire marriage with undiagnosed obsessive-compulsive disorder in which I was a nervous wreck half the time. I had given up a doctorate - nearly two doctorates, actually - and my partner. I grieved my 20s and much of my anxious teens. I had never felt normal, even as a child, and I was right. I was always in my head – I even used to get in trouble for it when I was in elementary school – and I had missed my life. I grieved the life that would have been. I would feel anger toward the people who had refused to "label" me AKA give me the correct diagnosis. I would feel anger at my partner for triggering the worst of the obsessions and anger at my parents for not getting me help as a child. I grieved times of not feeling so much anger. I grieved the life I would have had in those years.

Professionals historically struggle with how to classify experiences of grief. Labeling is important to understand this process, as grief can be so incredibly dysfunctional and life-altering. Two editions ago, the DSM would not diagnose anyone with depression if they were grieving a loved one. It was an important distinction. When the DSM-V was released, those who were grieving and met criteria for major depressive disorder could be diagnosed with the disorder. In the newest edition of the DSM, grief is its own diagnosis. For anyone who meets the criteria, to include the death of a loved one at least 12 months before, prolonged grief disorder is diagnosed.

Though grief and depression now stand as two different things, diagnostic grief is still only acknowledged to be after the death of a person. Not a pet, not a job, not health, and certainly not of time lost. And despite this 12-month criteria, most professionals now agree that a "normal" period of grief, in terms of a significant loss, is 1-2 years. Though grief is still something I cope with, anger a feeling I harbor when life is challenging, the most significant aspects of my own grief were in this 1–2-year timeline.

Happiness was coming, but I had to still unload a bucketload of emotions before I got there. Today, I am still getting there. Today, I have bad days, but I now have access to that once far-off emotion.

———————

One evening, I went to dinner with someone I had met working in Colorado. She told me about her older brother's diagnosis of autism spectrum disorder and how that affected every single day of her childhood. She talked about the weight her parents and siblings bear due to his incapacities, their inability to connect with him, and the difficulty in managing his outbursts at times.

She questioned the genetic implication this may have on her future children. She questioned if it was fair of her to pass the gene on, as she began to cry. And then, knowing my own experience with OCD which I had felt safe to share with her, she asked me if I ever also questioned if I should have children.

This was such a deep and honest question that I cried. Not just because I could relate to the question so intimately, but because I honored this person for being so honest, in a way that is so rare today. Most women would be offended for someone else to question if they should reproduce. But it is a real question we should all ask ourselves. It is natural, and beautifully authentic. It wasn't a judgment on her part, it was her own fear that she was sharing with me - and going a step further to ask if I shared her fear. If I could connect with this very intimate part of her.

And I do. In the past more so than now, I have even judged those who do not ask the question. Those who do not ask themselves – before having children – if they could really give their child a good life. If they themselves should be parents. How darkly honest of us to ask a question I've never heard anyone else really admit to asking: *should I pass on **me**?*

Well, no, I shouldn't. But this simple question does not have a simple answer. If I were guaranteed to have a child with severe OCD with my level of suffering, I would not have them. But statistically and logically, I'm almost *more* likely to not have a child like myself. Few of us have the same experiences as our parents.

The question of: *To create life or not* is one that reminds me of a friend I had in high school. He had stated multiple times, amid suffering from a psychotic disorder, that "his mother should have aborted him." And I think that at the end of the day, there are no guarantees and no sure things. I personally suffer from something that is far less genetic than Schizophrenia, early onset of Alzheimer's Disease, and Huntington's Disease but far more genetic than most mental illnesses.

I have a paternal uncle who we discovered had hoarded things after he had a heart attack at age 50. The hoarding was significant and being that it is an obsessive-compulsive disorder, this would probably be the genetic predisposition for my own OCD – a relative I never knew. My mother is anxious, and has obsessive personality tendencies, but nobody else has the diagnosis, and certainly nobody else has the lifelong symptoms that I have had.

I teach mental health, and I am not sure there is a topic that I have considered more so than the nature or nurture of mental health disorders. I have had patients who have no known genetic predisposition to things that are highly genetic, such as dementia or schizophrenia, though they suffer from them. At the end of the day, I believe all diseases have components of not only nature, but environment. If I were to blame something for my own diagnosis, it wouldn't be my genetics; it would be the support of compulsive tendencies in my young environment, and later, adult trauma. It would be my inclination to blame myself. It would be my intelligence and highly analytical mind. It would be my self-**doubt** and lack of trust that things will turn out for the best. But certainly not my genes.

What is important is the child who is born. Will they be a fighter? Soft-hearted or difficult to please? Impulsive and a little too adventurous? Will they be attracted to the "wrong" people? Perhaps parents, in a careful, intentional manner that is so rare today, can consciously choose not to support inclinations they themselves have and thus are more likely to pass on to their children. Thus, what is also important – and I claim, perhaps the most important – is the parents. That all are prepared to have, love, support the children they have. *Any* children they have.

I never want to be there again. I refuse to lose myself in my pain again. So, when it's me or the pain, I will always choose to be the person I know I am, which is the person I want to be.

I want to be a steady partner, the partner I am. I want to be the same kind of parent, which I will be. I will not force myself to think of my worst, because I know that I am not there. I know that

I will never be there again. Because I am here, and I refuse to choose there.

I want things I cannot control. Things that could be ripped from under me. It took me years to embrace uncertainty and learn to follow my heart over my head, and it is something I still work on. I can't control the future, I can't control my partner, and I had to be okay with that. I had to embrace the Now, my own happiness, not knowing if either of us would mess things up later. Not knowing if she would leave one day. Not knowing if my children would always be safe or happy. Not knowing if they would even outlive me. Nothing is sure.

Amanda will never be completely safe. She could hurt me. She could want something else. But I must trust my heart that she won't. And that if she does, it was meant to be and all worth it. Love is risk. Family is risk. Life is risk. To have the things I want, I needed treatment. I needed to accept uncertainty and **doubt**.

––––––––––––

Today, I remain on my medication. I have had one instance in which I thought I needed to switch. Before I did, I improved and then realized it was merely the stress of a new school year. I know my triggers, as everyone should, but there are always more coming. Sometimes I am fooled, sometimes I think I need to be doing more, but with time, I know I will always know the difference.

Planning to have a family, I recently attempted to come off my medication. It was a calm and happy time. I had just gotten married, and we were on a long vacation in Florida. Not the most stable time, but a happy one. In the short time I attempted to simply reduce my dosage, I began to get symptoms back. I didn't sleep as well, my anxiety rose, and I became more and more obsessive. I cried a lot. In this, I must say, that I had my **doubt**s that this way was the best course of action for either me or a child. How can a medication that helps to balance out the normal, necessary chemicals in my brain be of risk more so than the overwhelming anxiety and fear?

I live with the side effects whenever I forget my medication. I take my medication at night after determining this was the time of day in which I would feel the best effects of it. When I forget, I suffer a night of lucid dreaming – nightmares in which I cannot wake up, all night long. Sweating, anger, extreme anxiety upon waking. When this happens despite my efforts to remember, the side effects own about half my day until my late dose kicks in – mostly, I try not to interact with anyone. The side effects are so extreme that by the time I finally open my eyes, I know I missed my pill.

Here's the thing about OCD: we whose obsessive **doubt**ing and compulsing lies inside our minds, not always tangible…we look like everyone else. Our **doubt**ing looks like everyone else's **doubt**ing (though most will not admit this, there's plenty of research to support it). It's our *reactions* to the **doubt**ing that is not "normal," and certainly not functional.

About a year after I was hospitalized, still very much having bad days but also just as many good ones, I moved to Colorado. This was when I really did begin to move on. Being in the place where I was ill never felt happy to me, and if I wanted to get beyond just surviving, I knew I had to physically move.

In this time, I threw out my old self – the one plagued by internal turmoil. I threw out my clothing (which no longer fit anyways), I threw out any books I would not reread, I sold my house, I threw out my endless supply of ineffective herbal remedies, and most importantly, I threw out my journals.

These journals largely contained stream-of-consciousness writings I had collected in my years that I lived through what was happening inside my head. If I had a repetitive thought, it meant something. If I went to a psychic and they said something I didn't like, I obsessed – sometimes, for *years.* I compulsively got psychic readings, at many points in my journey. I was governed by thoughts, words, and predictions. These things aren't merely interesting or fun or even worrisome for me. They are dangerous.

Sometimes, I give in. Sometimes I argue with my mind. Sometimes I check things, and sometimes I cry or consider coming off my medication. Sometimes I even listen to the more despicable thoughts. But I do not act on my thoughts or my resulting fear. My career, our home, our family are everything to me. I don't watch movies or shows with a lot of drugs or promiscuity. By choice – it's not remotely interesting, yet it can be incredibly uncomfortable. And I do not make meaning out of that discomfort.

The thing that took the longest for me was self-trust. Given that those thoughts had become my world, that my guard was slowly beaten down enough to allow those thoughts to affect my beliefs, my attitudes, even my actions, I had lost any feeling of who I truly was. Even when I began to remember my true self, it would be years before I could say I trusted myself.

Today, I live in Colorado with Amanda and our dog and cat. We both teach, and we can understand and relate to each other's daily lives more than ever. We have a home with a backyard where our cat and dog sit each day, watching the leaves or snow fall, our dog always in one of the sweaters she loves. We have the seasons we always wanted, the peace and quiet that define us, and space to breathe. I am good friends with my ex-husband, who spends his career helping animals, as he always loved.

Living the life that you desire takes courage. So much courage, in fact, that most people never go through with it. Ten years ago, a younger me moved to Mississippi in the hopes of carving my own path, and I found that I lacked the strength, partner, and location to do so. Amanda had made similar moves prior, as well, always returning to the place that didn't quite feel like home. Fear never leaves, knowing what can happen in one's life on any given day. But if we choose, strength can overcome.

Aware

There is a very high correlation between a society repressing scientific theories and repressing freedom of speech, expression, exploration, thought, and development. Thus, it's critically important for any society to have courageous individuals willing to speak out in defense of these freedoms: these individuals usually pay a price for such statements but inspire people around them with the logic and decency of their claims, gaining momentum for change and reform.

Yuval Bar-Or

COVID-19 closures helped me tremendously. I had the space I finally needed to rest my mind and develop the coping mechanisms that eased my anxiety better than anything ever has. I began painting, and when I did, any anxiety I felt would dissipate. And when I began to breathe again in a way I hadn't known in years, I felt everything I hadn't been feeling in that time. I felt sadness, isolation, regret, and I began to grieve those things lost.

Amanda and I had a lot of downtime together to focus on our future, relearn each other after a traumatizing experience, and I was able to teach from the comfort of my home, with my animals and partner present. I could eat regular meals, it eliminated the physical burden of teaching while allowing me to still connect with students daily, and I spent more time with family.

Like any terrible experience, there is good too. I believe COVID-19 allowed people to realize more so what is important, spending more time with their families, spending less money, and thus needing less money, and taking better care of themselves. People realized working crazy hours for low-paying jobs and companies that did not appreciate them was not worth the sacrifices. The burden was on businesses to pay more money, with the risk of not attracting employees otherwise. We all realized that so much of our work could be done from home, without the necessity of spending time and money and energy on commutes. And to validate it all, people have ended up working more hours for their companies, overall costing the companies less, while being happier.

On the other hand, going from a significant trauma to COVID-19, there are negative effects too. Amanda and I moved during a pandemic, and after living in Colorado for two years, we have made very few connections. When my parents visit – largely, the only ones doing so – it is with two masks, five hours through the sky, taking a risk to see their daughters. Last year, not only was it the first one without the large Italian Christmas they have had for literally 40 years, but it was without both of their children – one who lived across the country and another who was sick with COVID-19.

Something born from the pandemic is the sense of isolation throughout our country and world. The feeling of deep separation from other people only enhances the poor state of mental health. Not only are people separated physically, but we are separated by our politics, values, cultures, and reactions. More people than ever have mental health diagnoses, and more people than ever are not getting the help that they need.

I think that going from being diagnosed with a severe mental illness to a separation from all people and friendships that I, for 29 years, had gained so much from, my end goal can't be fulfillment and happiness. Instead of the end goal being "happy," I feel that the realistic goal is *content*. I notice I am flatter, and I notice it in others as well. No matter how happy the day is, there is an underlying sadness. Not only did I lose so much, but right after, I joined the world in losing more. I think that in time, we are – as well as the generation being born into COVID - going to be biologically wired for sadness. Our children may not know the friendships, schools, and thrills that make up hearty childhoods.

———————

For every person who makes it, for every person who wins in the battle against their demons, there are those who perish.

I had a friend in high school who was bipolar. She was the first person I knew with this disorder, and certainly the youngest. She had been diagnosed when she was six years old after she jumped off a balcony to kill herself.

This friend was golden. She was an exceptional student, kind person, and she had everything going for her. She had a good family, and she could have done just about anything. When she told me, I was shocked. I could not see the illness in her, as if I expected it to leave physical signs. *3 percent of people are diagnosed with a bipolar disorder in their lifetimes.*

When I worked in adoptions, I saw brutal cases of victims who had suffered at the hands of untreated mental illness and substance use, most of the time triggering mental health issues in the children as well. One child had lived inside a cage for years. *1 in 7 kids will be abused or neglected in any given year.*

When I was 12 years old, a girl in my gym class told me that her stepfather was raping her. I will never forget how hard it was to convince her that there was help and that it had to change. That she deserved to live without this happening to her. She eventually went to the guidance counselor, and I decided I wanted to grow up to help the people who other people turn their backs on. *One in four girls suffer sexual abuse in childhood.*

I don't still have to know either of these friends, or where this child is now, to know their lives will never be the same. They will live with what happened to them for the rest of their lives. And if there comes a day in which they refuse to live with that terrible reality, they will self-destruct. They may even die. Self-destruction is nothing more than killing ourselves a little bit at a time, trying to forget.

One evening, I had a student walk into my office and shut the door. This was a young, male student, and he was trembling. He wouldn't meet my eye. I knew that whatever he was about to say would shake my world, and that it had shaken his for a long time. I took his hand, because that is the only thing I could do to tell him "I am here" without interrupting probably the hardest thing he's ever had to say. He said, "I have kept a secret for 20 years, and for the first time ever, I met someone who I want to tell, and that person is you." He went on to express that for years growing up, at the hands of another, he was forced to perform sexual acts with his sibling. To this day, it is one of the worst stories I have heard. And yet, I hear them all the time. How many people with mental health issues, undiagnosed, hurt children? How many of those children later kill themselves because they blame themselves and cannot live with the guilt, or the memories?

Mental health is less real to the world as it does not materialize before the eyes of other people. It's invisible. The suffering very much inside the heads of its victims. Because it cannot be witnessed, it will never be as real as physical illness. It does not matter how much suffering it causes or how many lives are changed forever. And that is the other difference. There are few serious physical ailments that are permanent, to be accepted and battled forever. Even in remission, if someone is lucky for its disappearance, the mental illness lingers. Its inhabitants, its victims must be careful of its appearance once again.

The first way we must begin to alleviate suffering and support those with mental health concerns is to become aware and to accept the existence of the illnesses themselves. Denial and shame will only further the issues. The taboo of discussions surrounding mental health topics hits all cultures, but minorities are even less informed of certain disorders and less likely to seek help.

A large barrier to diagnostic issues in OCD is the large skew between the reality and the perception. While the belief that bipolar disorders consist of ups and downs and that schizophrenia involves seeing things that aren't there, OCD is seen as cleaning too much. There is a much broader or more varied presentation in that of OCD and thus, the public image of it is much farther from reality. Further, due to the inherent **doubt**ing inside the disease, it is highly unlikely an individual will themselves know that they have an issue, no less, figure out on their own what that issue is. For this reason, even as a therapist myself in the world of mental health since I was 14 years old, it took me until the age of 29 to find my label – and even then, I lost it all over again when a therapist reinstilled **doubt** in my mind. Further, shame and stigma involved in taboo intrusive thoughts can lead to even less accuracy in diagnosis and treatment, further aiding the high misdiagnosis rate.

With the lack of professional knowledge, and thus lack of confidence in treatment, there are more people suffering undiagnosed than getting help. Given the high rate of OCD and the consequences of improper diagnosis noted above, professional education and less stereotypes surrounding OCD will give way to effective treatment.

Back to fundamental attribution error (the tendency for outsiders of a situation to overestimate the role of the actor's behaviors and underestimate situational causes), it is natural for individuals who do not suffer themselves to incorrectly put more blame on the person than on the situation. Mental illness, substance abuse, suicide, and violence are largely result from systemic issues rather than personal factors. Mental health is unquestionably a significant problem, and yet, too often, practitioners of all kinds diagnosing and/or treating mental illness are uninformed, uneducated, and unable to give the high-quality care that is needed for improvement and recovery. Further, it is malpractice for a doctor to not know the illness in which they diagnose or to ignore a patient's needs and instincts.

Misdiagnosis, fueled by the lack of mental health knowledge, is not unique to OCD, and begs a larger question: why is there such a lack of mental health knowledge, especially in the professional community? If we could uncover some causal factors to this detrimental pattern, perhaps the pattern can change. Perhaps, we can save lives. Knowing the misdiagnosis rates and gaps in knowledge, further research can begin to ask questions that work toward a remedy. What kinds of training are most effective in educating clinicians and the general population about OCD and other prevalent mental illnesses? Do clinicians know how to treat these disorders, and if not, how can we require further training to do so?

The diagnosis rate of Major Depressive Disorder went from 9% in 2004 to 17% in 2020. Though those with severe impairments in MDD have grown since 2009, the largest growth has been in the 18-25 age group, from 5.2% to 12.1%. This is also the hardest age to be at, for almost anyone.

More than half of this age group only had one parent or had parents who were divorced. Today, young people's main goal is to make money, while in 1971 this answer ranked #5, with goals such as helping others being in higher ranks. Due to these financial struggles, young people have different priorities than those in past generations – but with far less ability to accomplish these things. The goal of money may be a logical one, but unfortunately, following something for money will not usually lead to the same place as where your heart lies. Many individuals may wake up day after day miserable as they follow a goal that fails to fulfill and motivate them. And then they find out the hard way that they can't even attain *those things* that money allows. Despite higher costs of living, the average salary today is the same as it was 25 years ago.

To attain the desired things, one must sacrifice large portions of life. Gone are the days in which a man can get a sustainable job out of high school, have a family (and be able to support that family so his spouse can raise their children), purchase a home, and live the American dream. As a nation, we expect education, but we do not value it. Most developed countries fund higher education for their citizens – both for undergraduate *and* graduate degrees, but not here in America. *Though college graduates get a much higher wage on average than high school graduates, this is not because of a raise in either average income, but a decrease in income overall.*

As a PhD student, I was reminded daily of the things I had to do for future success, the long road ahead of me to attain a solid career…a career equally as respectable as the one my father could attain at 21…a career that my mother would never have had to think about. I was lucky to grow up with a stay-at-home mom raising me, and looking back, it meant everything that I always had someone right there helping me, driving me to school and dance class, and taking care of me when I was sick. We 20-something year-olds are faced with the impossibility of living on one income, the idea that having kids means giving our children to someone else 40 hours a week to raise. And all of this is assuming that, in this economy, we can get our much-needed jobs that we have trained for.

Not only do we have a new set of professional difficulties compared to past generations, growing up forces us to encounter evils that are only getting worse over time. I went to a brand-new high school and was part of the first graduating class, and on top of this and the school being rated an A-school, my friends and I still faced pressures and hardships such as an endless exposure to drugs, suicide, date rape, premature sex, self-harm, the fear of school shootings, and countless other things that have affected us all in different ways - things many parents didn't need to protect their kids from decades ago. Sure, many of us are successful on the outside, but this means nothing when compared to how damaged we may be on the inside. When volunteering in a psychiatric hospital a few years back, I came across a past classmate of mine who not only suffered from two very serious psychiatric disorders but was addicted to heroin and ecstasy. And he is not the exception anymore. He was 21.

Over time, crime levels increase. Drug use and premature alcohol use becomes unavoidable. Girls are more often experiencing puberty younger than ever before and the rate of pregnancy among our youth has increased. The lack of health education and the growing chokehold on women's rights and access to healthcare only increases the difficulties that young pregnant women face. Suicide rates escalate. And all these problems affect youth more than any other age group.

When accounting for the low incomes and high crime rates... it is easy to understand why 20% of adults today are living with mental illness – and 5% with *severe* mental illness. 15% of youth report suffering from a major depressive episode in the last year alone; most importantly, only 27% of youth with severe depression receive consistent care (constituted by only 7+ visits per year). These mental health issues include a major problem that is unique to our time: substance abuse – the largest issue for adolescents of our time. In fact, 7.74% of Americans are living with a substance use disorder.

The ability to talk about what we go through saves lives. Just recently, I strongly hesitated in mentioning to my dean that I was experiencing depression for only the second time in my life. *I hesitated.* Now, I am a social worker, therapist licensed in two states, have my doctorate in the field, and help people with mental health issues every day. I teach mental health. I've heard the worst of the worst. And I hesitated. And then, because we all need to change and *speak up* so that others can help, and because there is nothing wrong with it, I told her.

The isolation and secrets make for a recipe of going down a dangerous road. The suicide of Jason Altom – a Harvard grad school student – shocked the country in 1998 when he took his very precious, very talented life.

Every time I have known someone who has died by suicide or has lost someone by suicide, there is shock as people did not see it coming. But what experts know about suicide is that most of the time, there are signs, and it is not totally impulsive. People who take their own lives lose their purpose. Jobs have been lost, relationships ended, or mental health issues hit a breaking point. We cannot prevent the reaction to a trigger, but we can prevent the things leading up to it. The one thing all people can do is to have their loved ones know that they are a safe place, that they have purpose within the lives of those loved ones.

I conduct research on suicidality, and just recently, I was interviewing a research participant about his recent suicide plans. When I asked what had ended the cycle of the most recent attempts, he stated "this did."

Awareness saves lives.

Decades ago, the FDA mandated black box warnings on all antidepressants, notifying users that they increased the risks of suicide. Following such warnings, in the countries which applied these labels, diagnoses and prescriptions went down while suicide rates went up.

Even when it was shown in research that these increased suicide risks were mainly for children under the age of 25, and likely those who are inclined genetically to bipolar disorders (making antidepressants without mood stabilizers likely to trigger manic symptoms such as impulsivity), the FDA black box warnings were not removed from the packages of antidepressants. Why would we continue to warn against something that has saved countless lives, as thousands of studies have shown since? Now the people who need help only hear and see these warnings and lose a little bit more of the hope they did have.

We each may or may not come to the point in our lives where we just don't see the point anymore. When it's hard to carry on. Generally, when we express these feelings to others, especially those who have never experienced the same low before, they examine the situation that is making us this way. Not always to understand, but to subconsciously judge if it's worthy of these feelings. To come up with solutions that don't exist. People expect others to have these extreme emotions when houses burn down, people die, and when there are bad accidents. But it isn't always the horrible things that cause some of us to hit bottom, making it even harder for others to demonstrate empathy. Who would think that choosing the wrong graduate program would leave me with no will to live? The outside image of a situation does not determine the pain involved. When we feel that we are somehow stuck in life or in a situation, we hope for an out. Even things that we never wanted before suddenly become attractive if they serve a means to get away from our own suffering. As rates of mental illness continues to be on the rise, including the incidence of suicide, the ways that families and societies support mental health treatment, response, and awareness largely factors into the consequences of these illnesses.

———————

How would my life be different if it were free from OCD?
I would be free.
If I could, would I give OCD back? Would I take it all back?
I'm not sure, even now. But maybe not.

OCD has taken *me*. My self-love, identity, my time. My love – for anything I once loved….my job, my family, my life. My health. My image in the mirror, or in the eyes of others. My feeling of safety. A PhD. Joy. Probably many brain cells. My 20s. Some of these things, I got back. Some will never be the same. I will never again feel the same in a crowd or feel as connected to other people. And I cannot get the time back.

But for each thought of what OCD has taken from me, I remind myself of what it's given. Strength, beyond what I could have imagined. Wisdom. Patience and kindness. Gentleness. Caution. Clarity, of what is important. Knowledge, more than anything. That you just never do know what will happen. Knowledge, of the meaning of suffering. And awareness of how many people have, do, and will suffer.

Mental health is neither good nor bad. It is dynamic, changeable, and complicated. We are each different from one another and from our own mental health tomorrow. Some of us have sleep issues, anxiety, depression, psychotic symptoms, sexual issues, and dissociative symptoms. We all struggle at times, and not putting labels on it or words to it not only affects us. It isolates the next individual, too.

Let's own it and take away its power.

Alive

Things do not change. We do.

Henry David Thoreau

To talk about OCD, I must shake hands with a demon I have come to know.

We all have them. The things that keep us up at night, worried. The fears of what could happen, the memories of what has. Death. Sickness. Disaster. What will be, on the worst days of our lives.

My demon lives inside of me. It sounds like me, walks like me, and everyone else believes it is me. For most of my life, I believed it to be me, too.

But my demon is not my story. Every day, I not only make the choice to starve the demon and feed the life I deserve, but I also make a bigger, riskier choice. I choose to know this will be the choice every day of my life.

_____

Life is hard. *Really hard,* for some of us. And sometimes hard, for all of us. And what those of us who get better learn is that that does not change for anything. Not money, not relationships, not location, and not job. Amanda changed my life, not because she saved it – I did that. But because she made it worth it. If I had to knowingly guess at what my life would have been without her, I know this.

I would never have gotten as sick as I did. Because I had nothing for my OCD to take that was all that great. It wouldn't have reared the worst onto me because previously, it had nothing to destroy that was as important as her. But I would have been as sick as I always had been, as anxious, as unhappy, as fearful.

If I didn't have Amanda, I wouldn't have gotten better. I wouldn't have said "no, you are not winning, because this is *worth* me fighting, until the day I die, if I must. If it kills me, I will die fighting."

Another thing anyone who gets to the very edge of a cliff and leans over it, pondering, will tell you is that your mind does not see choices in that moment. It will only build on what you have been contemplating up until then. Moving to the wilderness of Wyoming, going to a hospital, or jumping from a cliff. When you are that sick, that unhappy, that truly **tormented,** you have no choice. There is choice every day until you get to that edge, but at that moment, there are no choices but the only thing your twisted, ill mind has already conspired.

For me, it was hospitalization. It was the day I decided that my survival had come to an end. It was the day I checked myself in with the sound of screams from my mother and grandmother and asshole therapist. The day I refused to leave until I saw a doctor. No visitors, please.

It was the day I very much gave up the love I had found. Because as far as I knew, and as far as Amanda felt, checking myself in without telling her was a goodbye. And I knew that. But

I could no longer be the best thing in her life, because I was no good thing.

I have had endless arguments about this "decision" I made. What most people – at least the healthy family I love – will hopefully never understand is that I had absolutely no choice. Because their daughter, fiancé, friend, granddaughter was disappearing and only shadows of her remained. I had to die to survive.

Healing is a positive word. It is also dark, unstable, indecisive, and full of fear. Knowing it had dragged me to the edge, I leapt in the opposite direction – to land – and hoped that before it would take over, I was healthy enough to fight back.

Obsessive-compulsive disorder, more than Amanda, more than my doctorate, more than my move across the country, and more than food and shelter, changed my life. Healing happens every day. I write this three years after the worst of it, and I am just now beginning therapy for what is left of that experience: trauma. Severe trauma. The kind that keeps me up at night and the kind that means I have far more nightmares than I would ever tell a client is normal and the kind that has strengthened some relationships while it has weakened most and that kind in which I know it could come back at any time.

But it cannot take me.

Healing is also smiles. It is getting kisses each day from my wife. It is cuddling with my dog. It is happy. It is happiness that I have never, ever known before now. It is planning for a child, and it is hobbies I have never been able to have. Work used to keep me sane, it was my only outlet, the only one that I could use to escape my head. Now I have painting and woodworking and puzzling and simply sitting on my couch and looking at the mountains out of my window.

And better yet, it is helping others. It is helping others in a way I could never feel the benefits of before. It is this instinct, this knowing that I didn't have before about what people need.

It is gratitude. That each day, I am me. I am bossy, and a super-introvert and all the things I am not proud of, but it is me. And that is worth everything.

———————

Once upon a time, I wrote a story of my life in five years. I was ill, lost in every way, and the only thing I knew is that I loved my partner very, very much. I wanted her, I wanted children with her, to live in a beautiful place with seasons and a house with a backyard for our animals. I wanted to be a professor and write a book. I wanted to be happy. But I had something that kept me from all of this. Something that, at the time, was nameless.

It has been five years, and today, I know its name, and most days, I have these things. Two years later, I am married and own a house in Colorado where I am a professor. Weeks ago, I was the Excellence in Teaching award recipient for my university. Happiness has always been a hard play for me (and isn't it a lot to expect of ourselves?), but I know this. I love what I do, work hard every day, and not only do I trust myself, but I *know* that I am trustworthy. Most importantly, to myself. And despite my vow to base my life on choice and not believe too much on "meant to be," this I know is true: this moment is meant to be.

I am strong. I am loved.

I do not survive, I live.

I am alive.

Other Resources

OCD Workbook. Hyman, B. M., & Pedrick, C. (2011). *The OCD workbook: Your guide to breaking free from obsessive-compulsive disorder.* New Harbinger.

Intuition and OCD. Penzel, F. (n.d.). *Ten things you need to know to overcome OCD.* Beyond OCD. https://beyondocd.org/expert-perspectives/articles/ten-things-you-need-to-know-to-overcome-ocd

Obsessive Compulsive Anonymous. https://obsessivecompulsiveanonymous.org/

Stahnke, B. (2022). *Recognizing and understanding obsessive doubting: Obsessive-compulsive disorder micro-course.* Walden University School of Lifelong Learning. https://lifelonglearning.waldenu.edu/recognizing-and-understanding-obsessive-doubtingobsessive-compulsive-disorder/WMCP1014.html

Notes

Prodromal

1. **Suicide:** The Regents of the University of Michigan. *Facts and statistics.* University of Michigan counseling and psychological services. https://caps.umich.edu/article/facts-and-statistics-0

Fear

1. **Relationship OCD.** Doron, G., & Derby, D. (2014). *Relationship OCD.* OCD Newsletter. https://iocdf.org/expert-opinions/relationship-ocd/

Residual

1. **Just Right OCD.** Reid, J., Storch, E., & Lewin, A. (2009). *Just right OCD fact sheet.* IOCDF.org. https://iocdf.org/wp-content/uploads/2014/10/Just-right-OCD-Fact-Sheet.pdf

2. **Suicide Mode:** Ruud et al., 2001 & Brudern et al., 2016, as cited in Brüdern et al., 2018: Brüdern, J., Stähli, A., Gysin-Maillart, A., Michel, K., Reisch, T., Jobes, D.A., Brodbeck, J. (2018). Reasons for living and dying in suicide attempters: A two-year prospective study. *BMC Psychiatry, 18*(234). https://doi.org/10.1186/s12888-018-1814-8

3. **MTHFR Gene.** Marcin, A. (2019). *What you need to know about the MTHFR gene.* Healthline. https://www.healthline.com/health/mthfr-gene#symptoms

4.   **OCD Workbook.** Hyman, B. M., & Pedrick, C. (2011). *The OCD workbook: Your guide to breaking free from obsessive-compulsive disorder.* New Harbinger.

Educate

1.   **DSM-V.** American Psychiatric Association. (2013). Obsessive-compulsive and related disorders. In Diagnostic and statistical manual of mental disorders (5th ed.). https://doi.org/10.1176/9780890425596.744053

2.   **DSM Updates.** Van Ameringen, M., Patterson, B., & Simpson, W. (2014). DSM-5 obsessive-compulsive and related disorders: Clinical implications of new criteria. *Depression and Anxiety, 31*, 487-493. https://doi.org/10/1002/da.22259

3.   **Prevalence.** Ocduk.org. (2020). World Health Organisation and OCD. https://www.ocduk.org/ocd/world-health-organisation/

4.   **OCD Study 1.** Wahl, K., Kordon, A., Kuelz, K. A., Voderholzer, U., Hohagen, F., & Zurowski, B. (2010). Obsessive-compulsive disorder (OCD) is still an unrecognised disorder: A study on the recognition of OCD in psychiatric outpatients. *European psychiatry: The Journal of the Association of European Psychiatrists, 25*(7), 374–377. https://doi.org/10.1016/j.eurpsy.2009.12.003

5.   **OCD Study 2.** Stengler, K., Olbrich, S., Heider, D., Dietrich, S., Riedel-Heller, S., & Jahn, I. (2012). Mental health treatment seeking among patients with OCD: Impact of age of onset. *Social Psychiatry & Psychiatric Epidemiology, 48*, 813-819. https://doi.org/10.1007/s00127-012-0544-3

6.   **OCD Study 3.** Glazier, K., Calixte, R.M., & Rothschild, R. (2013). High rates of OCD symptom misidentification by mental health professionals. *Annals of Clinical Psychiatry, 25*(3), 201-209.

7.   **OCD Study 4.** Glazier, K., Swing, M., & McGinn, L.K. (2015). Half of obsessive-compulsive cases misdiagnosed: Vignette-based survey of primary care physicians. *Journal of Clinical Psychiatry, 76*(6), e761-e767. https://doi.org/10.4088/JCP.14m09110

8.   **OCD Presentations.** McCarty, R.J., Guzick, A.G., Swan, L.K., & McNamara, J.P.H. (2017). Stigma and recognition of different types of symptoms in OCD. *Journal of Obsessive-Compulsive and Related Disorders, 12*, 64-70. https://doi.org/10.1016/j.jocrd.2016.12.006

9.   **Intuition and OCD.** Penzel, F. (n.d.). *Ten things you need to know to overcome OCD.* Beyond OCD. https://beyondocd.org/expert-perspectives/articles/ten-things-you-need-to-know-to-overcome-ocd

10. **Psychotic Misdiagnosis.** Leung, J.G., & Palmer, B.A. (2016). Psychosis or obsessions? Clozapine associated with worsening obsessive-compulsive symptoms. *Case Reports in Psychiatry*, 1-5. https://dx.doi.org/10.1155/2016/2180748

11. **Misdiagnosis Case.** Rohanachandra, Y.M., & Vipulanandan, S. (2019). A case of an unusual presentation of obsessive-compulsive disorder in an adolescent. *Asian Journal of Psychiatry, 43*, 34-36. https://doi.org/10.1016/j.ajp.2019.05.008

12. **Thought Sticking.** Radomsky, A.S., Alcolado, G.M., Abramowitz, J.S., Alonso, P., Belloch, A., Bouvard, M., Clark, D.A., Coles, M.E., Doron, G., Fernández-Álvarez, H., Garcia-Soriano, G., Ghisi, M., Gomez, B., Inozu, M., Moulding, R., Shams, G., Sica, C., Simos, G., Wong, W. (2014). Part 1—You can run but you can't hide: Intrusive thoughts on six continents. *Journal of Obsessive-Compulsive and Related Disorders, 3*(3), 269279. https://doi.org/10.1016/j.jocrd.2013.09.002

13. **Doubt.** Penzel, F. (n.d.). *Ten things you need to know to overcome OCD.* Beyond OCD. https://beyondocd.org/expert-perspectives/articles/ten-things-you-need-to-know-to-overcome-OCD

14. **Intrusive Thought OCD.** Chase, T., Wetterneck, C.T., Bartsch, R.A., Leonard, R.C., & Riemann, B.C. (2015). Investigating treatment outcomes across OCD symptom dimensions in a clinical sample of OCD patients. *Cognitive Behaviour Therapy, 44*(5), 365-376. https://doi.org/10.1080/16506073.2015.1015162

15. **PET Scans.** Dieter, E., Speck, O., König, A., Berger, M., Hennig, J., Hohagen, F. (1997). 1H-magnetic resonance spectroscopy in obsessive-compulsive disorder: Evidence for neuronal loss in the cingulate gyrus and the right striatum. *Psychiatry Research: Neuroimaging, 74*(3), 173-176. https://doi.org/10.1016/S0925-4927(97)00016-4

16. **Brain Differences.** Boedhoe, P.S.W., Schmaal, L., Abe, Y., Alonso, P., Ameis, S.H., Anticevic, A., Arnold, P.D., Batistuzzo, M.C., Benedetti, F., Beucke, J.C., Bollettini, I., Bose, A., Brem, S. Calvo, A., Calvo, R., Cheng, Y., Cho, K.I.K., Ciullo, V. Dallaspezia, S...Kathmann, N. (2018). Cortical abnormalities associated with pediatric and adult obsessive-compulsive disorder: Findings from the ENIGMA obsessive-compulsive disorder working group. *American Journal of Psychiatry, 175*(5), 453-462. https://doi.org/10.1176/appi.ajp.2017.17050485

17. **Obsessive Compulsive Anonymous.** https://obsessivecompulsiveanonymous.org/

Awaken

1. **Self-Defeating Personality.** Ruffalo, M. (2019). *Masochistic personality disorder: Time to include in DSM?* Psychology Today. https://www.psychologytoday.com/us/blog/freudfluoxetine/201903/masochistic-personality-disorder-time-include-in-dsm

2. **Borderline Personality Disorder.** Kreisman, J. J., & Straus, H. (2021). *I hate you, don't leave me: Understanding the borderline personality.* Perigee Books.

Heal

1. **Grief.** Hyman, B. M., & Pedrick, C. (2011). *The OCD workbook: Your guide to breaking free from obsessive-compulsive disorder.* New Harbinger.

2. **Diagnoses.** Reinert, M., Fritze, D., & Nguyen, T. (2021). *The state of mental health in America 2022.* Mental Health America.

3. **Prolonged Grief Disorder.** American Psychiatric Association Publishing. (2022). *Diagnostic and statistical manual of mental disorders: Dsm-5-Tr.*

Aware

1. **COVID-19.** Meakin, L. (2020). *Working from home means working longer hours for many.* Bloomberg. https://www.bloomberg.com/news/articles/2020-03-

23/working-from-home-means-working-longer-hours-for-many-chart

2. **Statistics.** U.S. Department of Health and Human Services. (n.d.). *Bipolar disorder*. National Institute of Mental Health. https://www.nimh.nih.gov/health/statistics/bipolar-disorder

3. **Statistics 2.** Centers for Disease Control and Prevention. (2022, April 6). *Fast facts: Preventing child abuse & neglect*. Centers for Disease Control and Prevention. https://www.cdc.gov/violenceprevention/childabuseandnegl ect/fastfact.html#:~:text=Child%20abuse%20and%20negle ct%20are%20common.,neglect%20in%20the%20United% 20States.

4. **Statistics 3.** Centers for Disease Control and Prevention. (2022, April 6). *Fast facts: Preventing child sexual abuse*. Centers for Disease Control and Prevention. https://www.cdc.gov/violenceprevention/childsexualabuse/f astfact.html?CDC_AA_refVal=https%3A%2F%2Fwww.cd c.gov%2Fviolenceprevention%2Fchildabuseandneglect%2 Fchildsexualabuse.html

5. **MDD.** Center for Behavioral Health Statistics and Quality Substance Abuse and Mental Health Services Administration U.S. Department of Health and Human Services. (2021). *Results from the 2020 National Survey on*

Drug Use and Health: Graphics from the Key Findings Report. Substance Abuse and Mental Health Services Administration. https://www.samhsa.gov/data/sites/default/files/reports/rpt35325/2020NSDUHFFRSlides 090821.pdf

6. **Salary.** Rogers, A.T. (2019). Human Behavior in the Social Environment, 5th ed. Routledge.

7. **Jason Altom.** Hall, S. S. (1998). Lethal chemistry at Harvard. *The New York Times.* https://www.nytimes.com/1998/11/29/magazine/lethal-chemistry-at-harvard.html.

8. **FDA Warning.** Brent, D. A. (2016). Antidepressants and Suicidality. *Psychiatric Clinics of North America*, *39*(3), 503–512. https://doi.org/10.1016/j.psc.2016.04.002